INTERACTIVE COMPUTING SOFTWARE SKILLS

Microsoft® Windows® 95

Kenneth C. Laudon
Azimuth Multimedia Productions, Inc

Evan Kantor

Irwin McGraw-Hill

Boston Burr Ridge, IL Dubuque, IA Madison, WI New York San Francisco St. Louis
Bangkok Bogotá Caracas Lisbon London Madrid
Mexico City Milan New Delhi Seoul Singapore Sydney Taipei Toronto

Irwin/McGraw-Hill

*A Division of The **McGraw-Hill** Companies*

Interactive Computing Software Skills
Microsoft® Windows®

This book is printed on acid-free paper.

4 5 6 7 8 9 0 CRS CRS 7 6 5 4 3 2 1

ISBN 0-07-038441-X

Editorial director: *Michael Junior*
Sponsoring editor: *Rhonda Sands*
Marketing manager: *James Rogers*
Project manager: *Richard DeVitto*
Cover designer: *Amanda Kavanagh*
Interior design: *Yvonne Quirk*
Development: *Jane Laudon*
Layout: *Evan Kantor*
Compositor: *Pat Rogondino*
Printer: *Courier Stoughton*

Library of Congress Cataloging-in-Publication Data

Laudon, Kenneth C., 1944-
Interactive computing software skills : Microsoft Windows 95 / Kenneth C. Laudon, Evan Kantor.
p. cm.
Includes index.
ISBN 0-07-038441-X
1. Microsoft Windows (Computer file) 2. Operating systems (Computers) 3. Interactive computer systems. I. Kantor, Evan. II. Title.
QA76.76.063L3678 1997
005.4'469--dc21 97-5548
CIP

http://www.mhhe.com

Contents

Contents (continued)

Preface

Interactive Computing: Software Skills Microsoft Office 97

The *Interactive Computing: Software Skills* series provides you with an illustrated interactive environment for learning introductory software skills using Microsoft Office 97. The Interactive Computing Series is composed of both illustrated books and multimedia interactive CD-ROMs for Windows 95 and each Office 97 program: Word 97, Excel 97, Access 97, and PowerPoint 97.

The books and the CD-ROMs are closely coordinated. The coverage of basic skills is the same in CDs and books, although the books go into more advanced skill areas. Because of their close coordination, the books and CD-ROMs can be used together very effectively, or they can each be used as stand-alone learning tools. The multimedia interactive CD-ROMs get you started very quickly on basic and intermediate skills. The books cover this material and then go farther.

It's up to you. You can choose how you want to learn. In either case the Interactive Computing Series gives you the easiest and most powerful way to learn Microsoft Office 97.

Skills, Concepts, and Steps

In both the book and the CD-ROM, each lesson is organized around *skills*, *concepts*, and *steps*. Each lesson is divided into a number of skills. The basic concept of each skill is first explained, including where that skill is used in practical work situations. The concept is then followed by a series of concise instructions or steps that the student follows to learn the skill. A *running case study* throughout reinforces the skill by giving a real-world focus to the learning process.

The Learning Approach

We have taken a highly graphical and multimedia approach to learning. Text, screen shots, graphics, and on the CD-ROM, voice, video, and digital world simulation are all used to teach concepts and skills. The result is a powerful learning package.

Using the Book

In the book, each skill is described in a two-page graphical spread (Figure 1). The left side of the two-page spread describes the skill, the concept, and the steps needed to perform the skill. The right side of the spread uses screen shots to show you how the screen should look at key stages.

Figure 1

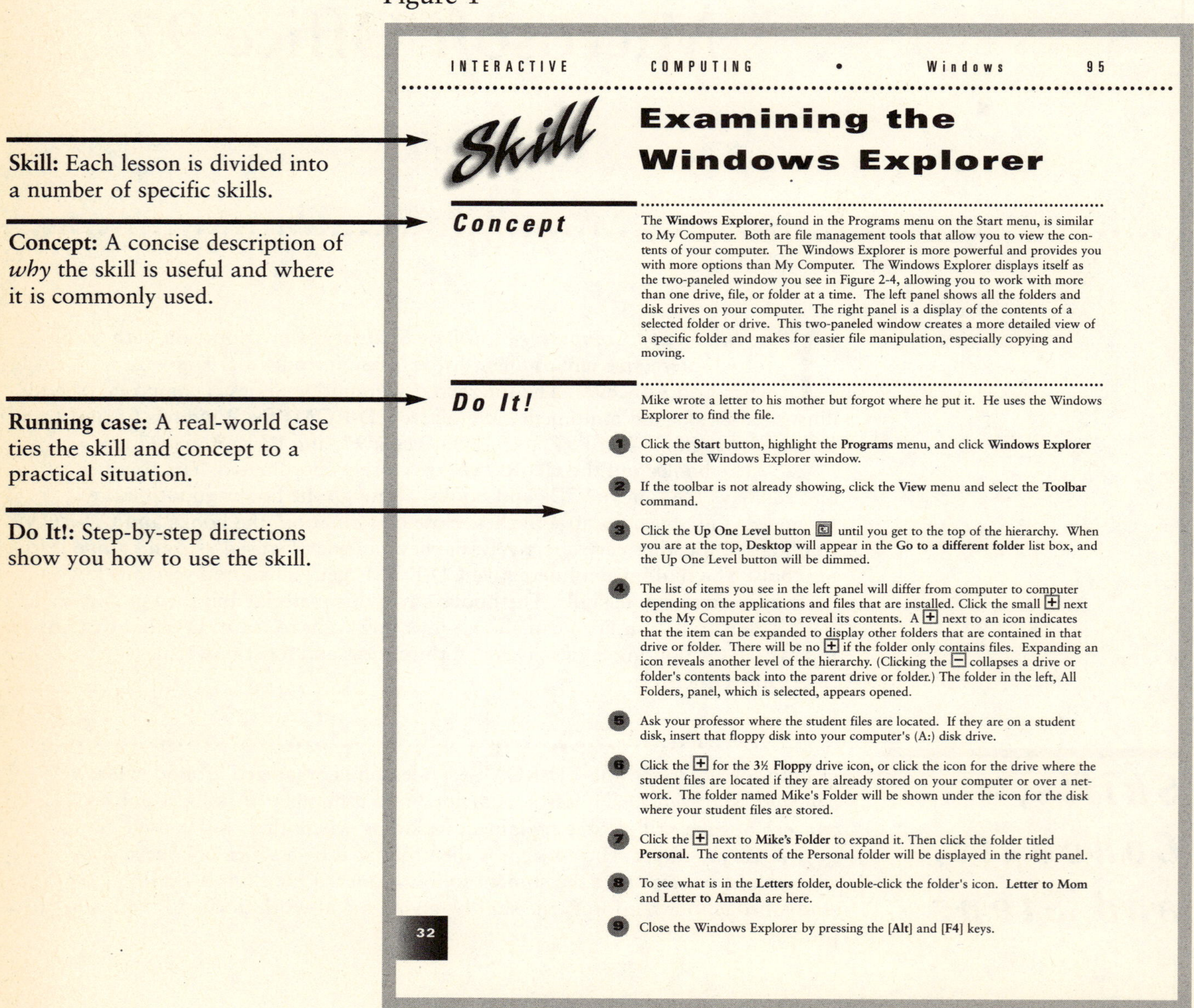

Skill: Each lesson is divided into a number of specific skills.

Concept: A concise description of *why* the skill is useful and where it is commonly used.

Running case: A real-world case ties the skill and concept to a practical situation.

Do It!: Step-by-step directions show you how to use the skill.

INTERACTIVE COMPUTING • Windows 95

Skill

Examining the Windows Explorer

Concept

The **Windows Explorer**, found in the Programs menu on the Start menu, is similar to My Computer. Both are file management tools that allow you to view the contents of your computer. The Windows Explorer is more powerful and provides you with more options than My Computer. The Windows Explorer displays itself as the two-paneled window you see in Figure 2-4, allowing you to work with more than one drive, file, or folder at a time. The left panel shows all the folders and disk drives on your computer. The right panel is a display of the contents of a selected folder or drive. This two-paneled window creates a more detailed view of a specific folder and makes for easier file manipulation, especially copying and moving.

Do It!

Mike wrote a letter to his mother but forgot where he put it. He uses the Windows Explorer to find the file.

1. Click the **Start** button, highlight the **Programs** menu, and click **Windows Explorer** to open the Windows Explorer window.
2. If the toolbar is not already showing, click the **View** menu and select the **Toolbar** command.
3. Click the **Up One Level** button until you get to the top of the hierarchy. When you are at the top, **Desktop** will appear in the **Go to a different folder** list box, and the Up One Level button will be dimmed.
4. The list of items you see in the left panel will differ from computer to computer depending on the applications and files that are installed. Click the small + next to the My Computer icon to reveal its contents. A + next to an icon indicates that the item can be expanded to display other folders that are contained in that drive or folder. There will be no + if the folder only contains files. Expanding an icon reveals another level of the hierarchy. (Clicking the − collapses a drive or folder's contents back into the parent drive or folder.) The folder in the left, All Folders, panel, which is selected, appears opened.
5. Ask your professor where the student files are located. If they are on a student disk, insert that floppy disk into your computer's (A:) disk drive.
6. Click the + for the 3½ **Floppy** drive icon, or click the icon for the drive where the student files are located if they are already stored on your computer or over a network. The folder named Mike's Folder will be shown under the icon for the disk where your student files are stored.
7. Click the + next to **Mike's Folder** to expand it. Then click the folder titled **Personal**. The contents of the Personal folder will be displayed in the right panel.
8. To see what is in the **Letters** folder, double-click the folder's icon. **Letter to Mom** and **Letter to Amanda** are here.
9. Close the Windows Explorer by pressing the [**Alt**] and [**F4**] keys.

32

End-of-Lesson Features

In the book, the learning in each lesson is reinforced at the end by a quiz and a skills review called Interactivity, which provides a step-by-step exercise and a real-world problem to solve independently.

Figure 1 (continued)

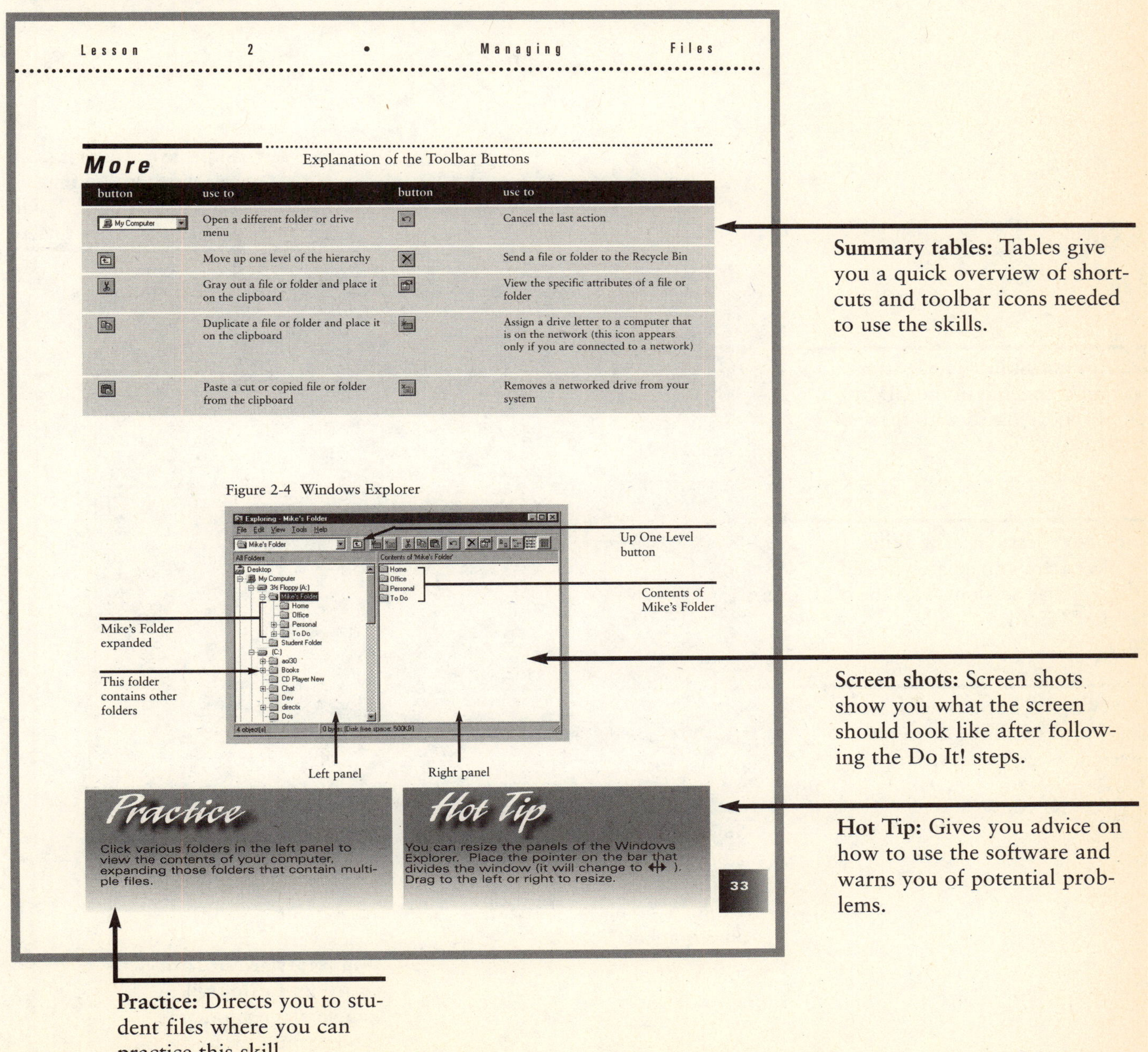

Lesson 2 • Managing Files

More Explanation of the Toolbar Buttons

button	use to	button	use to
My Computer	Open a different folder or drive menu		Cancel the last action
	Move up one level of the hierarchy		Send a file or folder to the Recycle Bin
	Gray out a file or folder and place it on the clipboard		View the specific attributes of a file or folder
	Duplicate a file or folder and place it on the clipboard		Assign a drive letter to a computer that is on the network (this icon appears only if you are connected to a network)
	Paste a cut or copied file or folder from the clipboard		Removes a networked drive from your system

Figure 2-4 Windows Explorer

Practice

Click various folders in the left panel to view the contents of your computer, expanding those folders that contain multiple files.

Hot Tip

You can resize the panels of the Windows Explorer. Place the pointer on the bar that divides the window (it will change to ↔). Drag to the left or right to resize.

33

Summary tables: Tables give you a quick overview of shortcuts and toolbar icons needed to use the skills.

Screen shots: Screen shots show you what the screen should look like after following the Do It! steps.

Hot Tip: Gives you advice on how to use the software and warns you of potential problems.

Practice: Directs you to student files where you can practice this skill.

Using the Interactive CD-ROM

The Interactive Computing multimedia CD-ROM provides an unparalleled learning environment in which you can learn software skills faster and better than in books alone. The CD-ROM provides a unique interactive environment in which you can learn to use software faster and remember it better. The CD-ROM uses the same lessons, skills, concepts, and Do It! steps as found in the book, but presents the material using voice, video, animation, and precise simulation of the software you are learning. A typical CD-ROM contents screen shows the major elements of a lesson (Figure 2).

Skills list: A list of skills permits you to jump directly to any skill you want to learn or review.

Figure 2

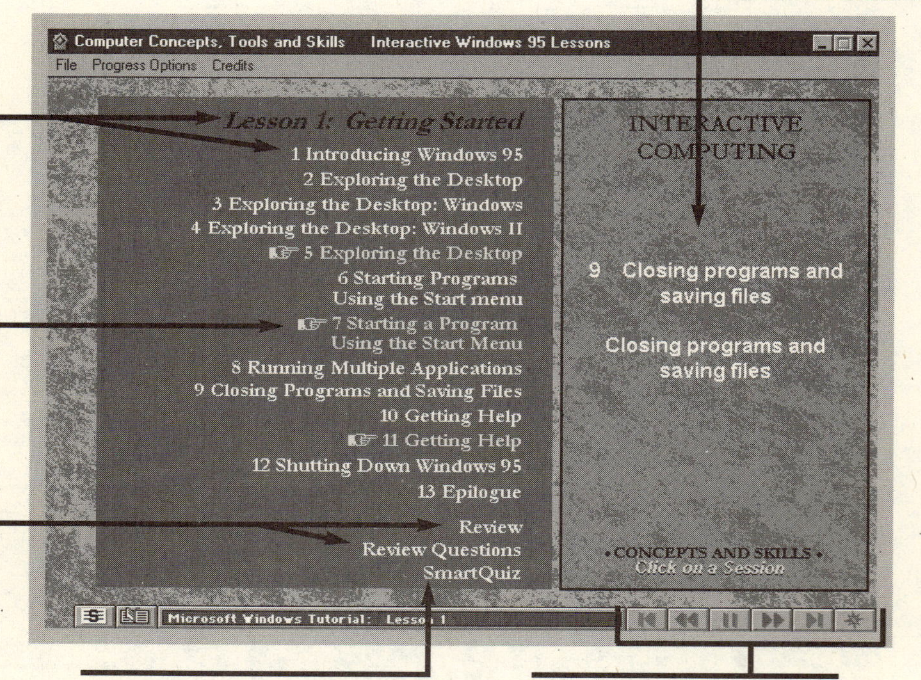

Lessons and skills: The lessons and skills covered in the CD are closely coordinated with those of the book.

Interactive sessions: The skills you learn are immediately tested in interactive sessions with the TeacherWizard.

Review: At the end of each lesson is a review of all the concepts covered, as well as review questions.

SmartQuiz: Each lesson has a SmartQuiz that tests your ability to accomplish tasks within a simulated software environment.

User controls: Precise and simple user controls permit you to start, stop, pause, jump forward or backward a sentence, or jump forward or backward an entire skill. A single Navigation Star takes you back to the lesson's table of contents.

Unique Features of the CD-ROM: TeacherWizards™ and SmartQuiz™

Interactive Computing: Software Skills offers many leading-edge features of the CD-ROM currently found in no other learning product on the market. One such feature is *interactive exercises* in which you are asked to demonstrate your command of a software skill in a precisely simulated software environment. Your actions are closely followed by a digital TeacherWizard that guides you with additional information if you make a mistake. When you correctly complete the action called for by the TeacherWizard, you are congratulated and prompted to continue the lesson. If you make a mistake, the TeacherWizard gently lets you know: "No, that's not the right icon. Click on the Open File icon at the left side of the toolbar on top of the screen." No matter how many mistakes you make, the TeacherWizard is there to help you.

Another leading-edge feature is the end-of-lesson SmartQuiz. Unlike the multiple choice and matching questions found in the book quiz, the SmartQuiz puts you in a simulated digital software world and asks you to show your mastery of skills while actually working with the software (Figure 3).

Figure 3

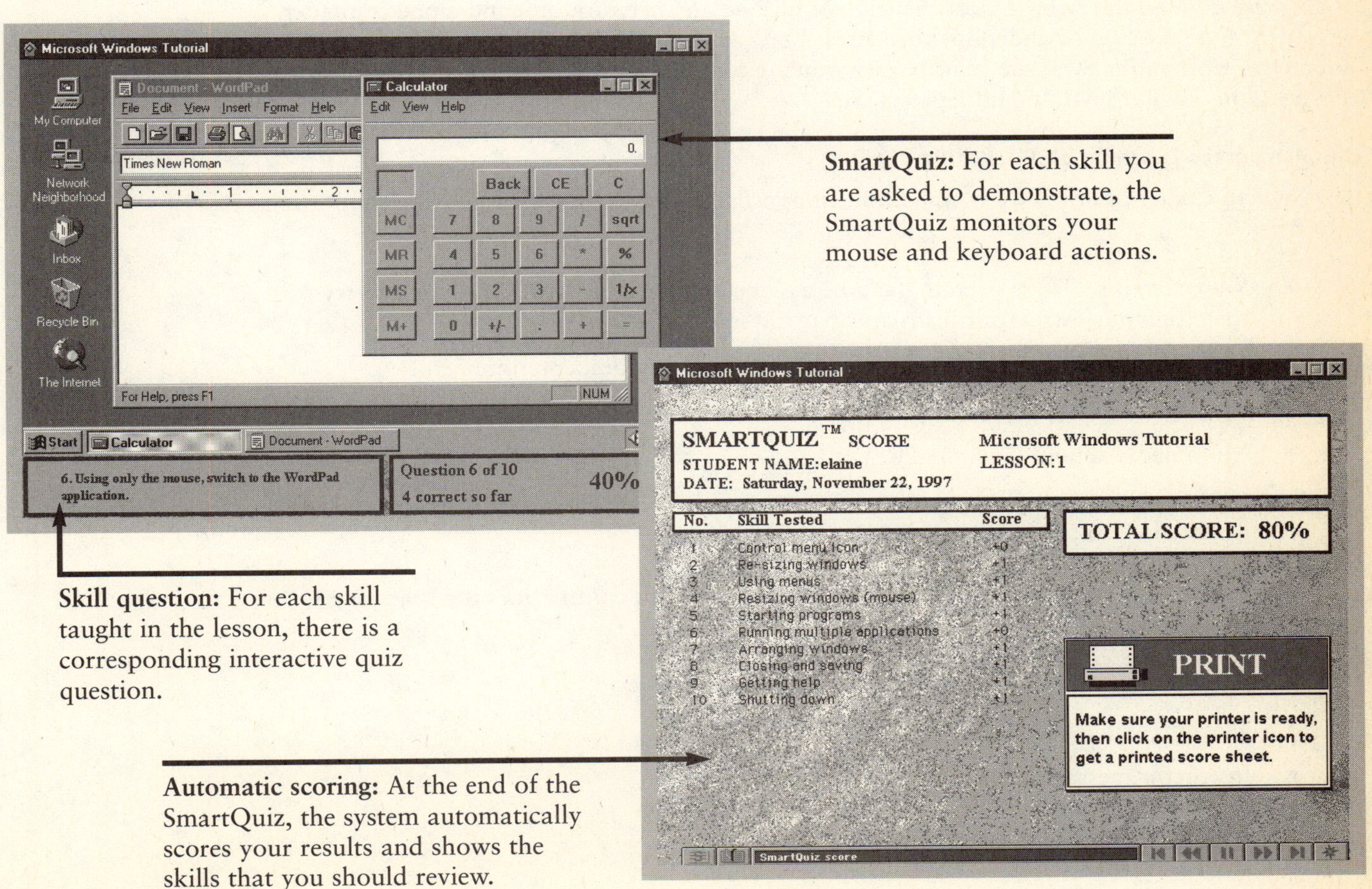

Using the CD-ROM and the Book Together

The CD-ROM and the book are designed to support each another. There is a close correspondence between the lessons and skills taught in the book and the CD for introductory levels of the software (Lessons 1 through 4), as well as between the case study used in the CDs and the books. Generally, the books have more lessons and go farther into advanced topics than the CD does, while the CD-ROM demonstrates the basic steps in more detail. Here are tips on using the CD and accompanying book together:

- You can use the book and the CD together at your student lab workstation or at home. Place them side by side and follow along in both at the same time.
- You can use the book when you do not have access to a computer, and use the CD by itself at school or at home.
- You can use the CD first to gain a quick understanding of the software, then use the book later at home or school ro review and deepen your understanding.

Student Files

The *Interactive Computing: Software Skills* books require that students have access to accompanying student files for the practice and test sessions. The instructor and students using the texts in class are granted the right to post the student files on any network or stand-alone computer, or to distribute the files on individual diskettes. You can download the student files from the Interactive Computing Web site at **http://www.mhhe.com/cit/apps/laudon/**, or request them through your Irwin/McGraw-Hill representative.

Supplementary Learning and Teaching Tools

The Student Center at http://www.mhhe.com/cit/apps/laudon/ provides the following supporting information:

- Web exercises: These exercises can be assigned by your instructor. Or you can try them on your own. Your instructor has the solutions.
- Cool sites: Web news, new technology, Web opportunities, entertainment.
- Message board: Talk to other students who are using the series.
- Multimedia action: Cool demos.
- Course help: Choose the course you're enrolled in. Then choose exercises, multimedia demos, free software, or course information.

The Faculty Lounge at http://www.mhhe.com/cit/apps/laudon/ provides the following instructional support:

- Exercises and solutions
- Teaching strategies
- Instructor message board
- Multimedia action
- Cool Web site
- Course help

Local Area Network Testing Facility

McGraw-Hill and Azimuth Multimedia have designed and produced a revolutionary and unique Network Testing Facility™ (NTF) that tests acquired software skills in a safe, simulated software environment. Operating on a network, the NTF permits students to take a self-paced exam from their workstations at home, at school, or in the classroom. The NTF automatically tracks student scores, and allows the instructor to build screens that indicate an individual student's progress or which skills may need more emphasis for the entire class.

Contact your McGraw-Hill representative for further information on the NTF.

Acknowledgments

The Interactive Computing Series is a cooperative effort of many individuals, each contributing to a team effort. Our goal is to provide students and instructors with the most powerful and enjoyable learning environment using both traditional text and new multimedia techniques. Achieving this goal requires the contributions of text authors, multimedia screenplay writers, multimedia designers, animators, graphic artists, editors, computer scientists, and student testers.

Our special thanks to Frank Ruggirello, who envisioned and initiated the Interactive Computing Series. Peter Jovanovich and Gary Burke of McGraw-Hill management generously supported a technological leap into the future of teaching and learning. Rhonda Sands, our editor, has gently pushed us to higher levels of performance and encouraged us to do the best we can.

- ▶ Exploring the Desktop: Icons
- ▶ Exploring the Desktop: The Mouse
- ▶ Exploring the Desktop: Windows
- ▶ Using Menus
- ▶ The Start Button and Starting Programs
- ▶ Using Dialog Boxes
- ▶ Running Multiple Programs
- ▶ Saving Files and Closing Programs
- ▶ Getting Help
- ▶ Shutting Down Windows 95

L E S 1 S O N

INTRODUCTION TO WINDOWS 95

Windows 95 is an **operating system** that controls the basic functions of your computer, such as loading and running programs, saving data, and displaying information on the screen. Operating system software is different from application software, such as a word processor or spreadsheet program, which you apply to letter writing or calculating data. Instead, operating system software provides the **user interface** — the visual display on the screen that you use to operate the computer by choosing which programs to run and how to organize your work. Windows 95 offers a **graphical user interface** or **GUI** (pronounced "gooey") that presents you with pictorial representations of computer functions and data.

It is through these pictures, or icons, that you interact with the computer. **Data files** are represented by icons that look like pieces of paper, and can be organized into groups called **folders**, which look like manila folders. The **My Computer** icon, represented by a small desktop PC, allows you to organize these files and folders. Other icons allow you to run programs such as a word processor or a paint program.

Windows 95 is a powerful operating system that allows you to perform a variety of high-level tasks. Windows was designed around the metaphor of a desktop in an office, and using it is similar to working with paper files and folders. Multitasking lets you run more than one application at once, easily switch from application to application, and share information among them. Included programs called **accessories** can be used to help you with day-to-day tasks. The **Find** feature quickly locates folders and files, and **Help** offers fast tutorial and troubleshooting advice.

Windows 95 is easy to use and can be customized with the preferences and options that you desire. This book will teach you about the basic elements of Windows 95 and how to use them. You will learn file management, advanced functions, and some of the special features of Windows 95. Throughout this text you will follow Mike Harwood, a small business owner, who is using Windows 95 for the first time.

Skill Exploring the Desktop: Icons

Concept

The main screen you see when you start Windows 95 is called the **desktop.** Figure 1-1 displays the Windows 95 default desktop. Do not be surprised if your desktop does not look exactly like the one pictured here as computers and their setup vary from machine to machine. The appearance of your desktop and windows will depend on the software installed and the configuration of various settings. Like the desk that you are sitting at, this screen is the work space on which all actions are performed. On the left side of your screen you will see small pictures called **icons.** Icons are pictorial representations of a task, program, folder, or file. Each icon represents an application that you can start. You double-click an icon to open an application.

The desktop features six icons: **My Computer**, **Network Neighborhood**, **Inbox**, **Recycle Bin**, **The Internet**, and **Set Up the Microsoft Network**. The **My Computer** icon is a tool you can use to organize your drives and printers. The **Network Neighborhood icon** allows you to work with computers and printers that you are connected to over a local area network. Using **The Inbox**, **The Internet**, and **Setup the Microsoft Network**, you can install software that will allow you to receive faxes on your computer, use e-mail, and connect to online services, provided you have the appropriate hardware. The **Recycle Bin icon** represents an area that stores deleted files. Across the bottom of the desktop is the **Taskbar**. The Taskbar shows you which programs, if any, are currently running. When a program is **minimized**, its icon only appears on the Taskbar. At the left of the Taskbar is the **Start** button Start. This button calls up a special menu that allows you to open programs, find files, get help, and more.

Figure 1-1 Windows desktop

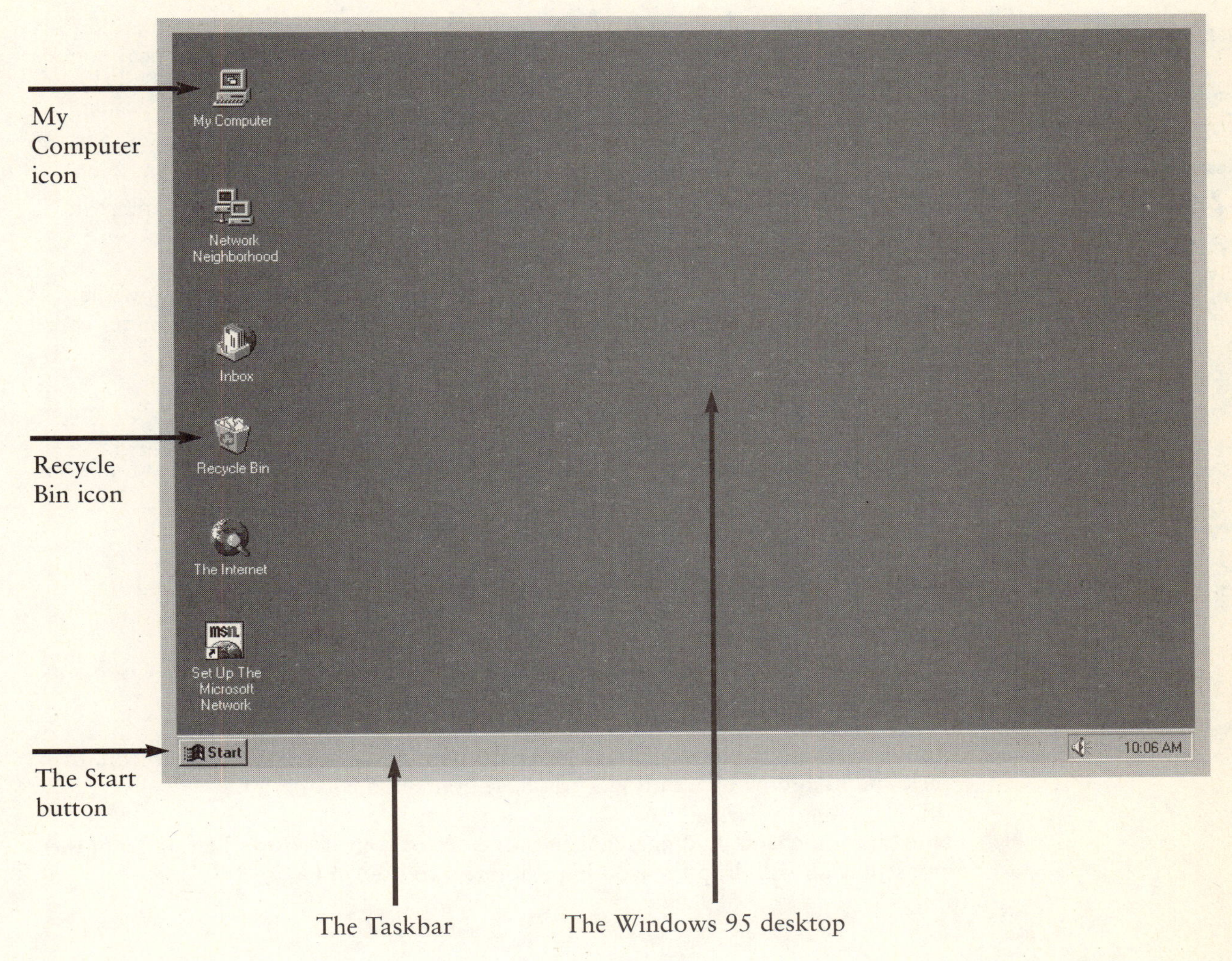

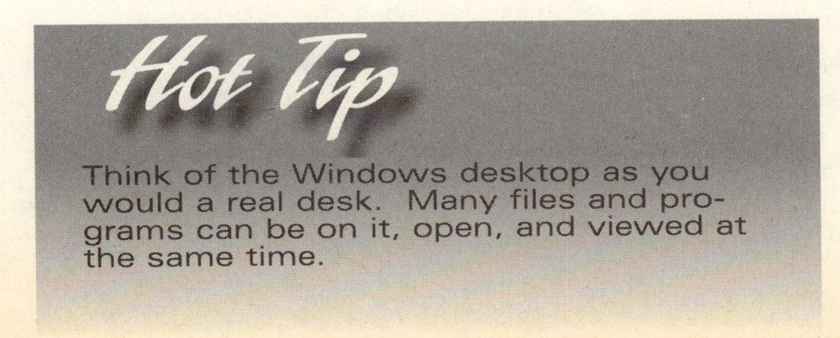

Skill: Exploring the Desktop: The Mouse

Concept

The mouse (Figure 1-2) is a hand-controlled input device that, when connected to the computer and moved along a clean, flat surface, will move the graphical pointer around the screen. The buttons on the mouse are used to give commands. There are three basic ways you can use the mouse: **clicking**, **double-clicking**, or **dragging.**

Do It!

Mike uses the mouse to move the pointer around the desktop and explore its functions.

1. Using the mouse, move the pointer around the desktop to get a feel for how the pointer moves in relation to the motion of the mouse. Positioning the pointer over an item is called pointing.
2. Locate the **My Computer** icon on the desktop. Place the pointer on the icon and click the **left mouse** button once. This will highlight the icon, indicating that it has been selected to perform a function. Click anywhere else on the screen to undo this action.
3. Double-clicking is done to open a program, file, or window. To open the My Computer application, place the pointer on the icon and quickly click the **left mouse** button twice. The My Computer window will appear on the desktop.
4. To close the window you have just opened, position the pointer over the **Close** button in the upper right corner and click the **left mouse** button.
5. Icons can be moved by dragging. Move the pointer to the **My Computer** icon, then click and hold down the button. You have grabbed the icon.
6. Now move the icon by dragging it to the center of your desktop. Letting go of the mouse button will drop the icon in position as you see in Figure 1-3.

Figure 1-2 A mouse

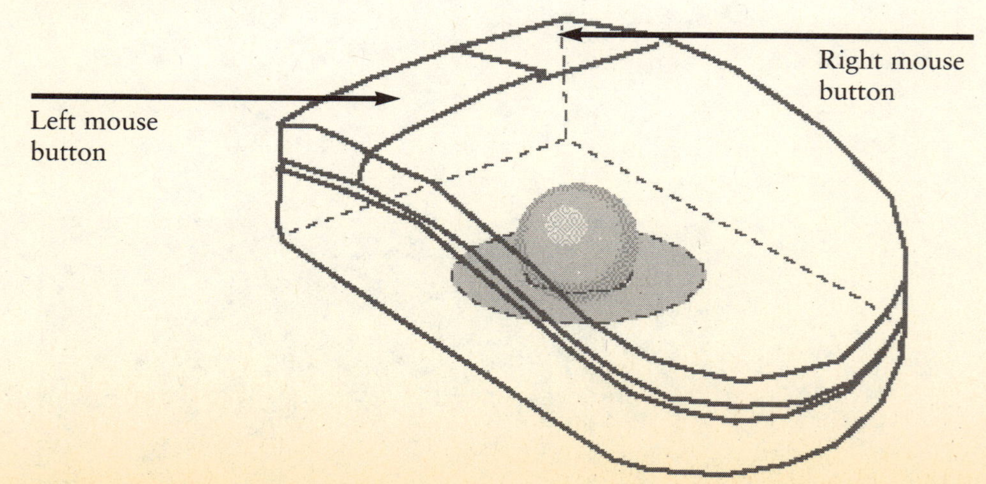

More

Basic Mouse Functions

mouse action	definition	use
Pointing	Positioning the pointer over an item on the desktop	Preparing to select an icon or other desktop item
Clicking	Pressing the left mouse button once to highlight an item	Selecting an item
Dragging	Positioning the pointer over an item, clicking and holding the left mouse button, moving the mouse, and then releasing the button	Moving an icon or other object to another location on the desktop
Double-clicking	Pressing the left mouse button twice in rapid succession	Opening an item or program to see its contents
Right-clicking	Pressing the right mouse button	Opening a pop-up menu of commands

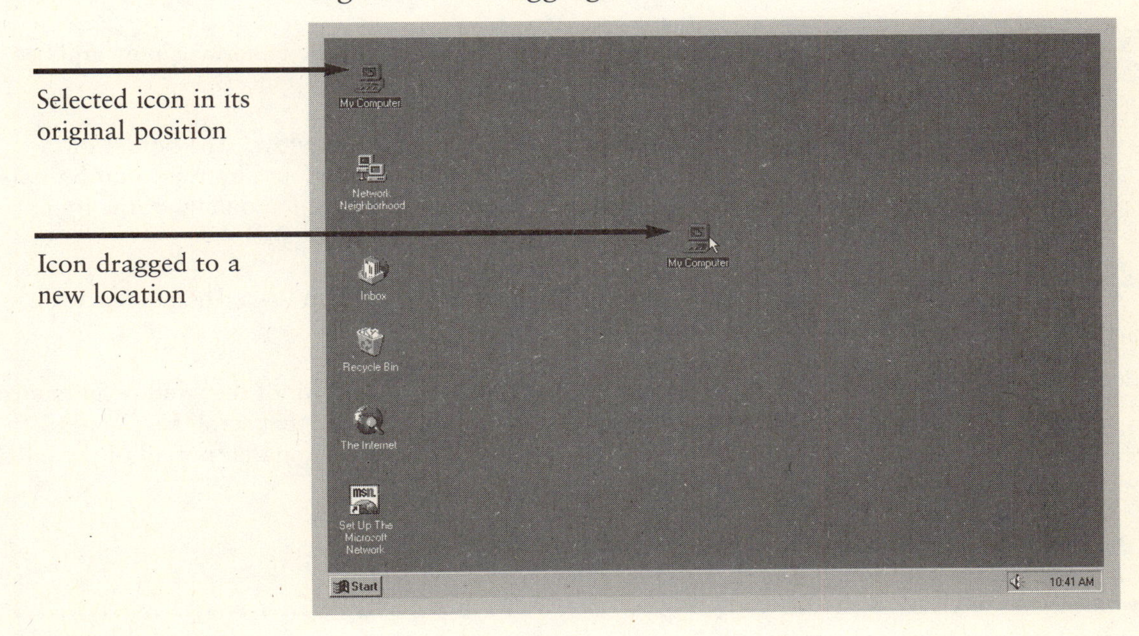

Figure 1-3 Dragging an icon

Practice

Open the Recycle Bin window by double-clicking the Recycle Bin icon. Close the window by clicking the Close button [X] in the upper right corner.

Hot Tip

Position the pointer in the middle of your screen and then pick up the mouse and place it on the middle of your mouse pad so you will not run out of mouse movement area.

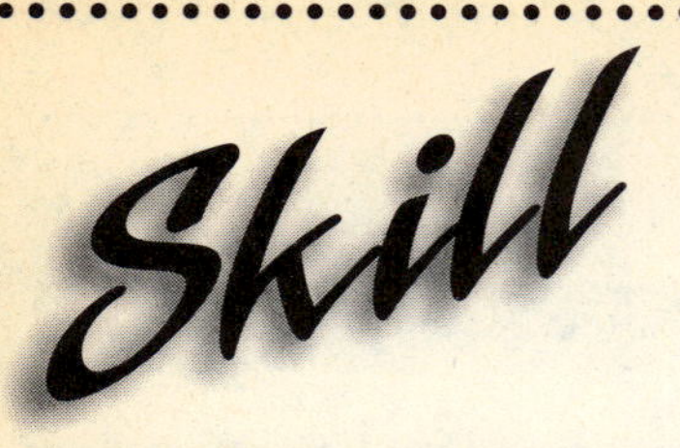

Exploring the Desktop: Windows

Concept

An **application** is a software program that is used to perform a specific task. A software program must be **open** and active in order for you to use it. When a program is opened, it forms a **window** or on-screen frame. Windows are flexible. They can be moved, resized, reshaped, and even hidden.

Do It!

Mike wants to open, move, and resize the **My Computer** window.

1. Double-click the **My Computer** icon. This will open the My Computer window.
2. To move the window, first click and hold the left mouse button with the pointer on the **title bar**, the blue bar at the top of the window that contains the name of the program (see Figure 1-4). Then, with the mouse button depressed, drag the window to the center of the desktop.
3. Place the pointer on the right edge of the window. This will change the indicator to a double arrow ↔.
4. Click and hold the left mouse button. The border of the window is now grabbed and can be resized.
5. Drag the edge to the right to increase the size of the window. The border of the window moves with the double arrow. Let go of the mouse button to drop the edge of the window into place. This action can be repeated on any of the four sides of the window to enlarge or decrease the window's size.
6. Place the pointer in the lower right corner of the window. The pointer will change to a diagonal double arrow ↘ .
7. Drag the corner up to decrease both the height and width of the window in tandem and to cover part of the icons in the lower row. Notice that **scroll bars** appear along the right and bottom sides of the window, indicating that not all of the information can be seen at once.
8. Leave the window open for the next skill.

More

When a window is too small to display all of its information, **scroll bars** will appear on the right and/or bottom edges of the window. Scroll bars are context-sensitive objects and only appear when the situation is appropriate. The scroll bars, shown in Figure 1-4, are used to slide information inside the window so you can see additional contents of the window. If you need to scroll slowly, or only a short distance, click a **scroll bar arrow** located at the end of the scroll bar. The scroll bar box indicates where you are located in the window. Clicking above or below the **scroll bar box** moves the display in large increments. Dragging the scroll bar box allows you to control the slide of the window's information.

Figure 1-4 A moved window

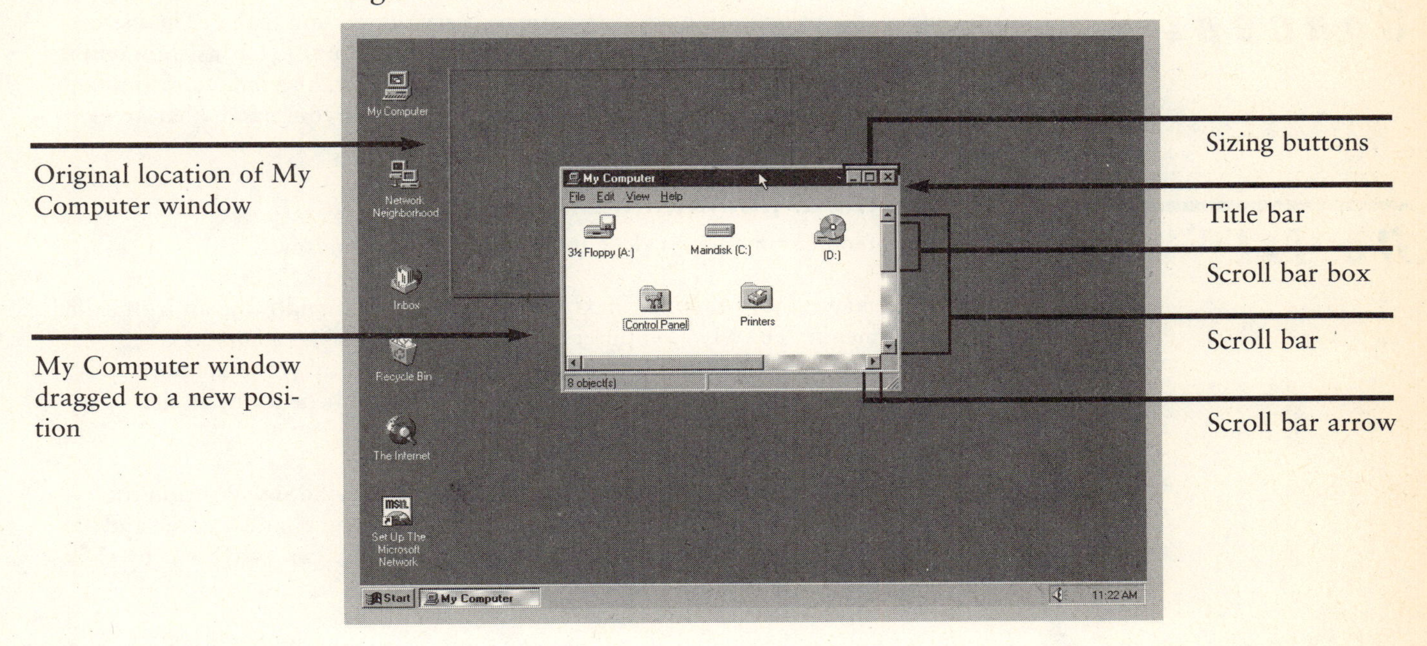

Sizing Buttons

sizing buttons		use
Maximize	☐	Enlarging the window so that it fills the entire screen, with the Taskbar remaining visible
Restore	🗗	Returning the window to its previous size
Minimize	_	Shrinking the window so it only appears as a program button on the Taskbar
Close	☒	Closing a window or program

Practice

Open and maximize the Recycle Bin window using the sizing buttons. Then restore the window and use the scroll bars to view all the window's contents. Close the window when you are done.

Hot Tip

You can maximize or restore a window's size by double-clicking the title bar.

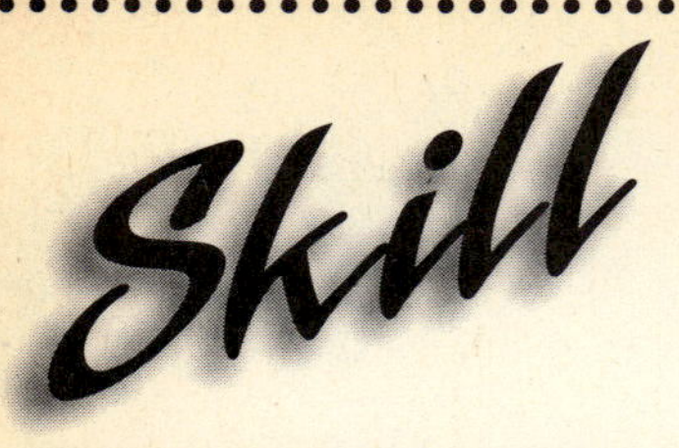

Using Menus

Concept

A **menu** is a list of operations that you use to carry out certain tasks. The list of menus is situated on the **menu bar** and is located under the title bar as shown in Figure 1-5. Each Windows program has its own menu list, and many are similar. Clicking on a menu item will produce a drop-down list of **commands** that are grouped according to function.

Do It!

Mike uses menu commands to close the My Computer window.

1. On the left side of every title bar, next to the name of the window, is an icon called the **control menu.** The My Computer control menu looks like a small PC. Move the pointer over the control menu icon and click to open the menu. A gray rectangle containing six commands appears on the screen beneath it, as shown in Figure 1-6.

2. The first five commands relate to resizing or moving the window. Position the pointer over the dimmed **Restore** command. The command changes color and becomes highlighted. Once a command is highlighted, you can activate it by clicking it — if it is not dimmed.

3. Continue to move the pointer down the list. Each command will be highlighted as you go. Notice that each command is accompanied by text that appears in the gray status bar at the bottom of the window. The text gives you a brief description of the function of the command.

4. Move the pointer over the **Close** command to highlight it. Click this command to close the My Computer window. The window will shut, leaving the My Computer icon highlighted.

More

Menu Conventions

item	definition	Example
Dimmed command	Indicates that a command is not currently available	Cut Ctrl+X
Ellipsis	Indicates that a dialog box will open	Save As...
Keyboard shortcut	A combination of keys that will execute the command	Print... Ctrl+P
Underlined letter	A single key that will execute the command; the [Alt] key must be used with the key if the item is on the menu bar	Full Screen

Figure 1-5 My Computer window

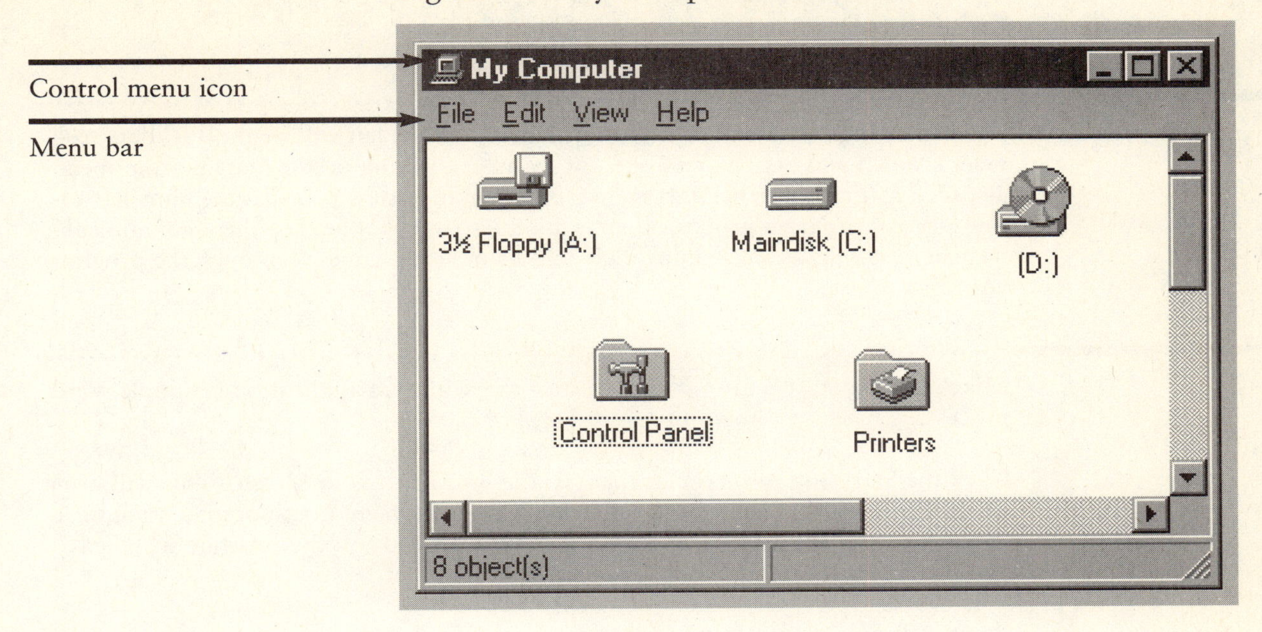

Figure 1-6 Control menu

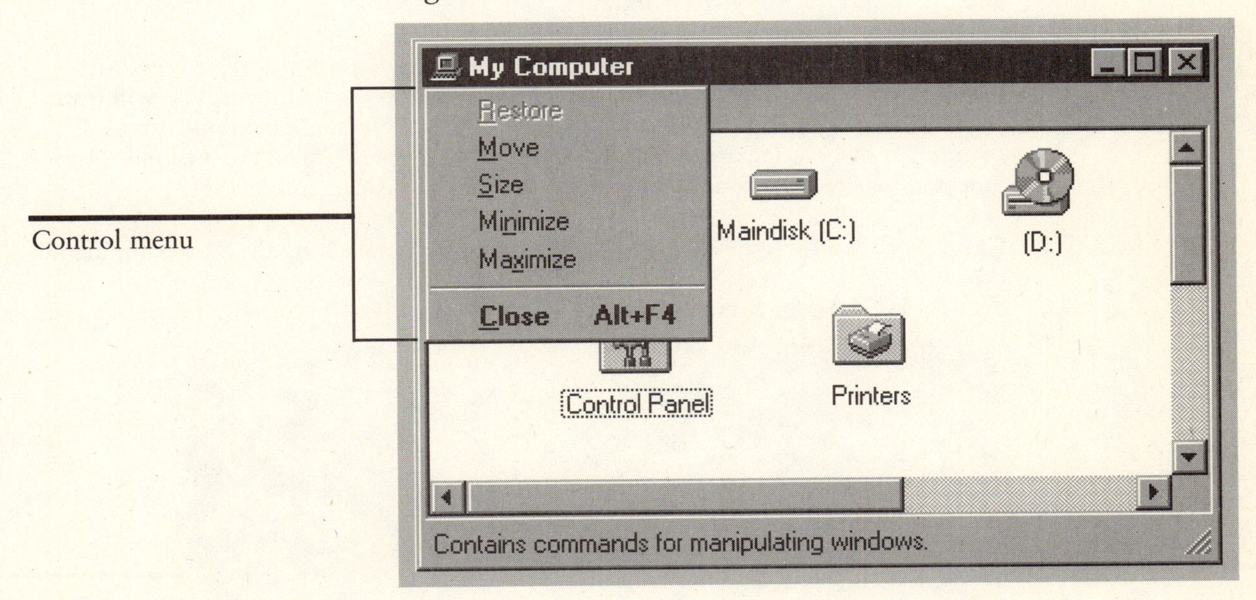

Practice

Open the My Computer window by double-clicking its icon. Use the Close command from the File menu to close the window.

Hot Tip

Once a menu is opened, you can use the arrow keys [↑,↓]to move from command to command or [→, ←] to move from menu to menu. You can select a menu command and perform its action by pressing [Enter].

The Start Button and Starting Programs

Concept

The Windows 95 **Start** button Start, located on the left side of the Taskbar, provides a quick and easy way to open programs. Clicking on the **Start** button opens a special menu called the **Start** menu, as shown in Figure 1-7, that contains left-to-right lists of program groups. Items with an arrow [▶] next to them contain submenus. Pointing to an item highlights it; a simple click will then open the program you wish to use.

Do It!

Mike uses the Start button Start to start the WordPad application (a simple word processing program shown in Figure 1-8).

1. Click the **Start** button on the Taskbar at the bottom of your screen. This will bring up the Start menu. Don't be surprised if your Start menu does not match Figure 1-7 exactly. The appearance of your Start menu depends on the software installed and the shortcuts created on your computer.

2. Point to **Programs** (notice the little arrow) to bring up the Programs menu.

3. Next, point to **Accessories**. These are applications that come with Windows 95 and are useful for everyday work.

4. Move the pointer to **WordPad**, which is located at the bottom of the Accessories menu, and click the **left mouse** button to start the application. WordPad will open with a blank file (Figure 1-8) as its default window. Open applications reveal themselves by creating a program button Document - WordPad on the Taskbar. An indented program button indicates that the program is currently active.

5. Close WordPad by right-clicking the **title bar** and then clicking the **Close** command.

Figure 1-7 Accessories menu

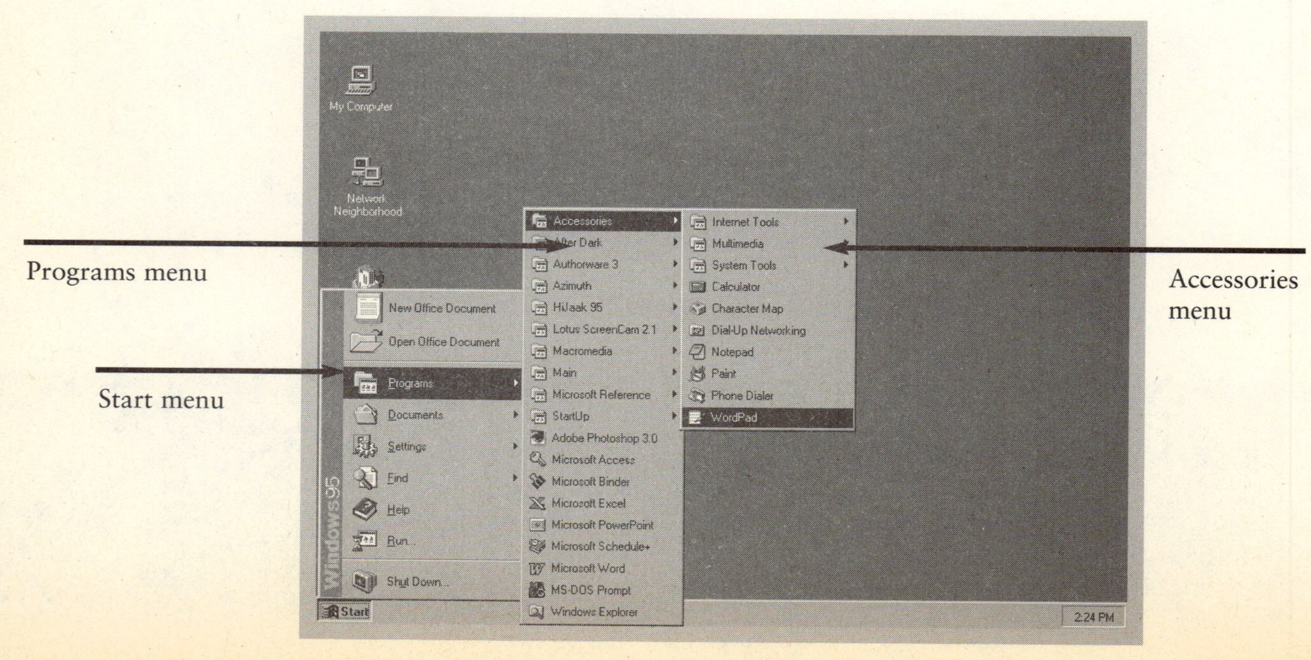

More

The Start Menu Categories and Items

menu / item	description
Programs	Contains numerous applications that can be opened from the Start menu
MS-DOS Prompt	Opens a window that allows you to use DOS commands
Windows Explorer	Activates the Windows Explorer, a file management tool
Documents	Opens the most recently used files
Settings	Allows you to change the default settings for the Control Panel, printers, and Taskbar
Control Panel	Contains icons that allow you to customize your Windows setup
Printers	Lets you install the files needed for connecting to a printer and to view the status of a file being printed
Taskbar	Provides a dialog box with options for altering the Taskbar and adding or removing Start menu programs
Find	Locates a program, file, or folder you are searching for
Help	Calls up the Windows 95 Help system
Run	Opens a program, folder, or file that you select by typing its name
Shut Down	Provides you with various options for ending your Windows session

Figure 1-8 WordPad window

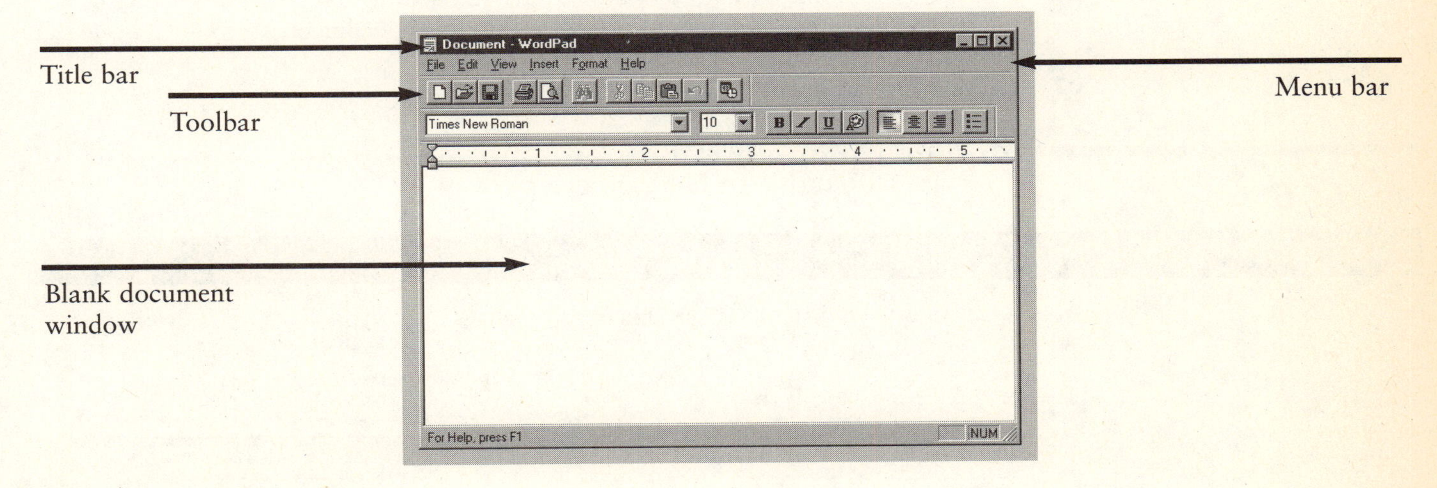

Practice

Use the Start button to open the Printers folder on the Settings menu. A window displaying the printers hooked up to your computer will appear. Close the window with the Close button [X] on the title bar.

Hot Tip

The Start menu can be customized. Programs can be added or removed to suit your needs. You will learn how to do this in Lesson 3.

Using Dialog Boxes

Concept

Commands that require additional information open a dialog box when selected. A dialog box allows you to designate the options you want to use. Located below the menu bar is the **toolbar**. The toolbar contains buttons that activate shortcuts to frequently executed commands. Pausing the pointer on a toolbar button will provide you with a **ToolTip**, a brief description of the button's function.

Do It!

To explore dialog boxes Mike will open WordPad, type his name, and insert today's date into a document.

1. Click the **Start** button, highlight **Programs,** then **Applications,** and, finally, click **WordPad.** WordPad will open with a blank document window as it did before.

2. To add text to a new document, all you need to do is begin typing. Type **Mike Harwood** and then press [**Enter**].

3. Click **Insert**, on the menu bar, to produce the Insert drop-down menu as shown in Figure 1-9. This menu item allows you to put different pieces of data into a document.

4. Click **Date and Time....** A dialog box like the one in Figure 1-10 will appear in the center of your screen, giving you various choices of date and time formats.

5. The month/day/year format is WordPad's default setting and is already selected. Click the **OK** button to insert today's date into your document.

6. Leave WordPad open for the next skill.

More

Items Unique to Dialog Boxes

item	definition	example
Tab	Similar to a paper file card; used to switch between entries in a dialog box	Index
Check box	A square that is clicked to toggle an option on or off	☑ Toolbar
Text box	A box with a cursor in which text is typed	File name: type text here
Radio button	A circle that is clicked to select a dialog box option	◉ Inches
Command button	A rectangular button that is used to execute a command	Apply
Drop-down box	A box with a down arrow that produces a list of choices	Down ▼

Figure 1-9 Drop-down menu

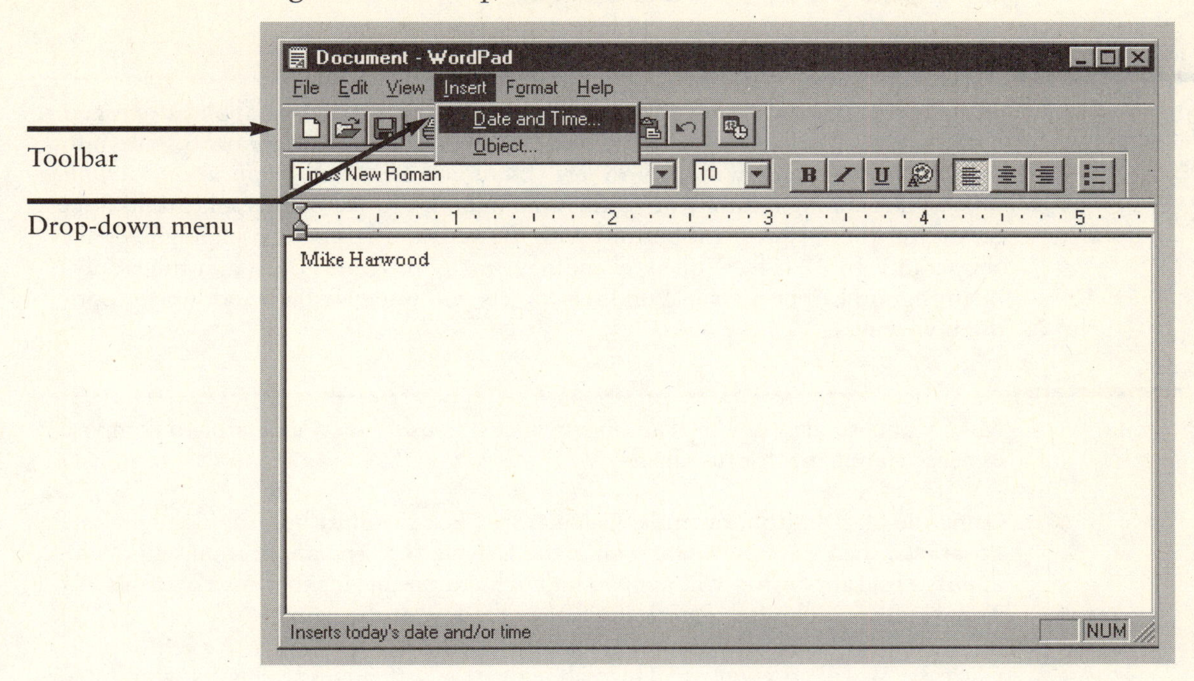

Figure 1-10 Date and Time dialog box

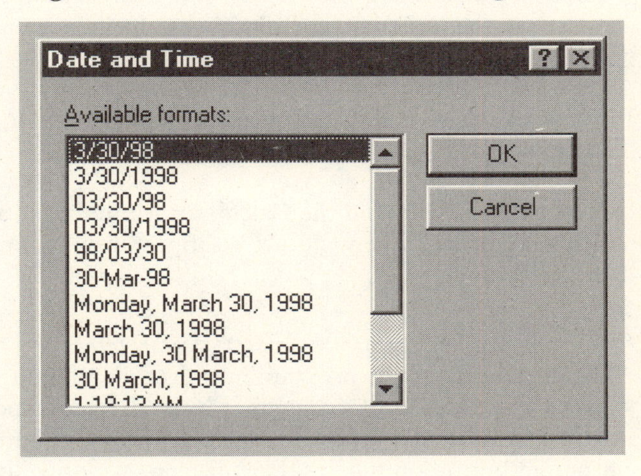

Practice

Open the Font dialog box from the Format menu. View the fonts by clicking through the font options. The sample area will show you what the typeface (another word for font) looks like. Then, close the Font dialog box .

Hot Tip

In a dialog box with more than one option you can move from option to option with the Tab key.

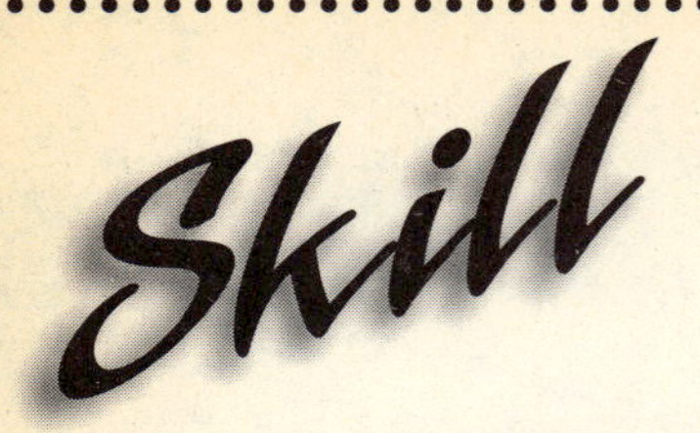

Running Multiple Programs

Concept

There are occasions when you will want to have more than one application open at once, either to view data from one file while working on another or to share information between files. Windows 95 lets *you move easily from application to application* while running **multiple programs** simultaneously. All open applications appear on the Taskbar as program buttons with the active program icon highlighted, as shown in Figure 1-11. While you can have many programs open at a time, only one program can be active. Windows 95 lets you organize the windows for optimum viewing.

Do It!

Mike wants to view a WordPad document while using the Calculator to compose expense statements for his clients.

1. Using the Start button, open the Calculator: Click the **Start** button, highlight **Programs**, then **Accessories**, and click the **Calculator**. The application will open and its program button will appear, highlighted, on the Taskbar next WordPad's. The windows will overlap with the active window at the front.

2. Click the **WordPad** window. This will activate WordPad and bring its window forward. The WordPad title bar will also become highlighted while the Calculator title bar becomes dimmed. A highlighted title bar indicates an active window.

3. You can also activate a window by clicking its program button. Click the **Calculator** program button on the Taskbar. To create space for the WordPad window, drag the Calculator by its title bar to the lower right corner of the screen.

4. Restore and then resize the WordPad window using the techniques learned earlier in this lesson, so you can view as much of the window as possible. Your desktop will look like Figure 1-12.

5. Click the **WordPad** and the **Calculator Minimize** buttons [-] to minimize the application windows. The windows disappear, leaving only their representative buttons on the Taskbar.

More

The Taskbar contains program buttons that tell you what programs are currently open. The applications can either have an open window on the desktop or they can be minimized — showing only as a program button. Clicking an application's program button on the Taskbar opens its window. If you want to hide an application, knowing you will need it later, it is best to minimize the window, placing it on the Taskbar for easy opening.

The Taskbar can also be used to organize your windows. When you right-click an open space on the Taskbar, a pop-up menu will appear. This menu lists the options that pertain to the way your windows will lie on the desktop. **Cascade** overlaps the windows and allows you to see only the title bars. The active window is put on the top of the pile and can be viewed in full. **Tile Horizontally** stacks the windows one above the other. **Tile Vertically** arranges the windows side-by-side. Both tile functions divide the desktop by the number of open applications to determine the size of each window.

Figure 1-11 Two open applications

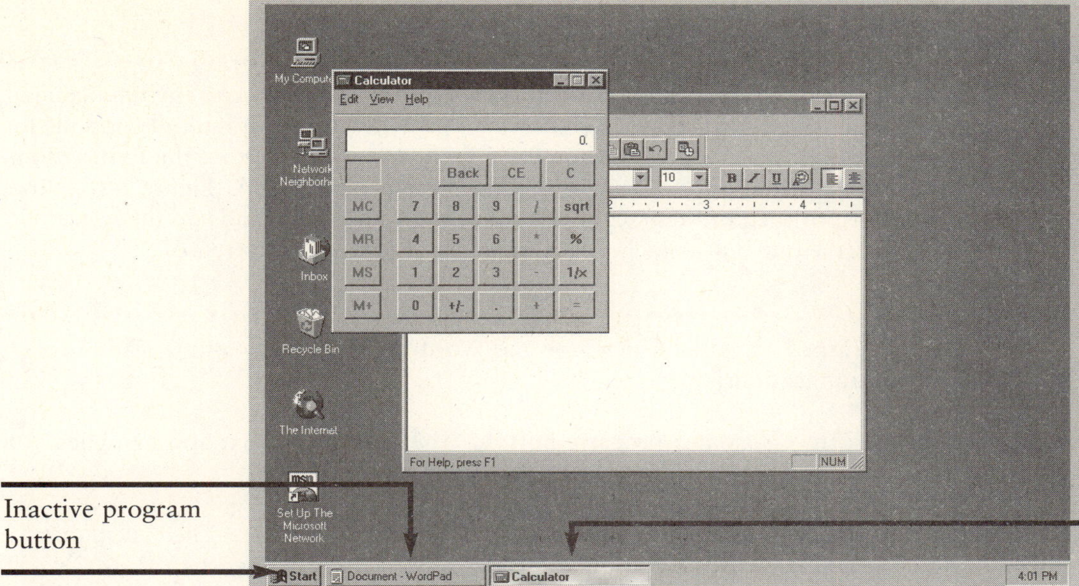

Figure 1-12 Resized windows

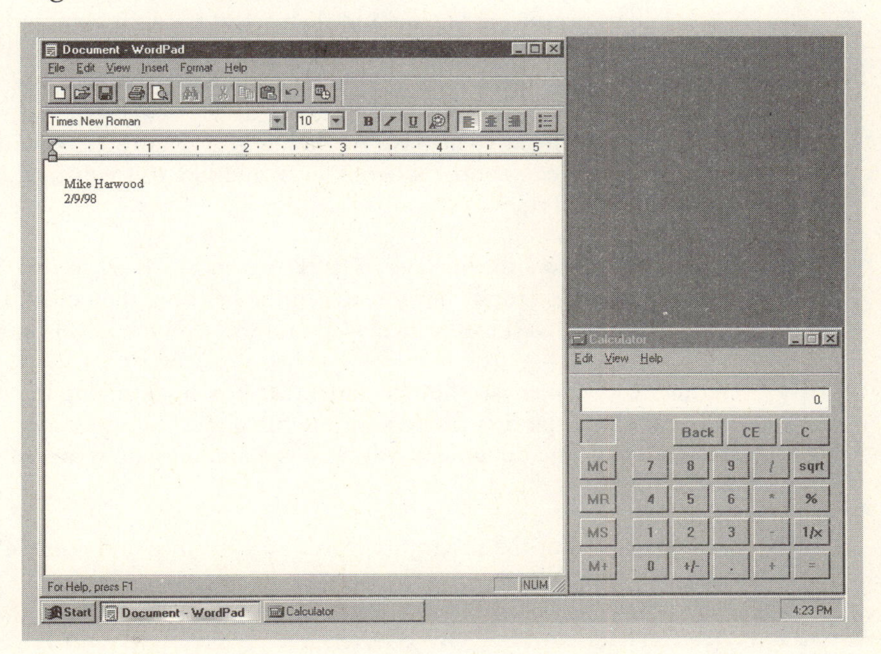

Practice

Click the Calculator program button on the Taskbar, then the WordPad program button, to alternate between active accessories.

Hot Tip

All open windows can be reduced to their program buttons on the Taskbar with the Minimize All Windows command.

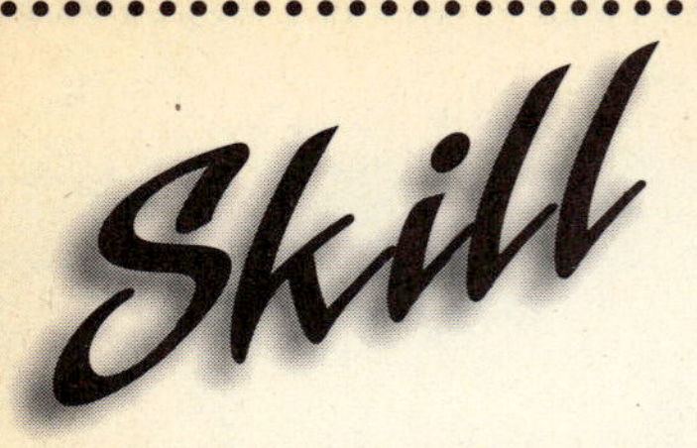

Saving Files and Closing Programs

Concept

Programs need to be properly saved and closed so you do not lose any data created during your Windows session. Windows 95 provides you with multiple options for closing a file or an application. You can use the Close [X] button, the Exit option from the File menu, or the Close option from the program icon. Figure 1-13 shows the location of each of these features. All of the Close commands do the same thing, and the one that you choose is a matter of personal preference.

Do It!

Mike is finished using the Calculator and WordPad for the day and is ready to close the applications.

1. Right-click the **Calculator** program button. The same menu that appears when you click the control menu will pop up.
2. Use the pointer to highlight **Close**. Click the **left mouse** button. The Calculator will close and its program button will remove itself from the Taskbar.
3. Click the **WordPad** program button on the Taskbar. The WordPad window will become active with the document Mike created in the window.
4. Click File to produce its menu and then select the **Exit** command. Because you have an open document that was not saved, WordPad will ask if you want to save these changes by opening a small dialog box with Yes, No, and Cancel buttons.
5. Click the **Yes** button. The **Save As** dialog box (Figure 1-14) will appear. In this dialog box you can choose where you would like to save your document and what you want to call it.
6. Desktop is selected in the **Save In** list box; this is where you will save this document. If the Desktop is not already in the list box, then click the **Up One Level** button until Desktop is displayed and the Up One Level button is dimmed.
7. Highlight Document in the **File name** text box by dragging the cursor over the entire word. Type **first file** to save the file under a useful name. Then click the **Save** button. The document will be saved and an icon representing the file will be placed on the desktop.
8. Click **Exit** to shut the program. WordPad will close and remove itself from the desktop.

More

Some applications, such as Calculator, do not have a File menu. These programs can be closed from the title bar by either selecting the Close command from the control menu or clicking the Close button. The control menu is the icon that appears on the far left edge of the title bar. Right-clicking anywhere on the title bar will also cause the control menu to drop down.

Figure 1-13 Options for closing a window

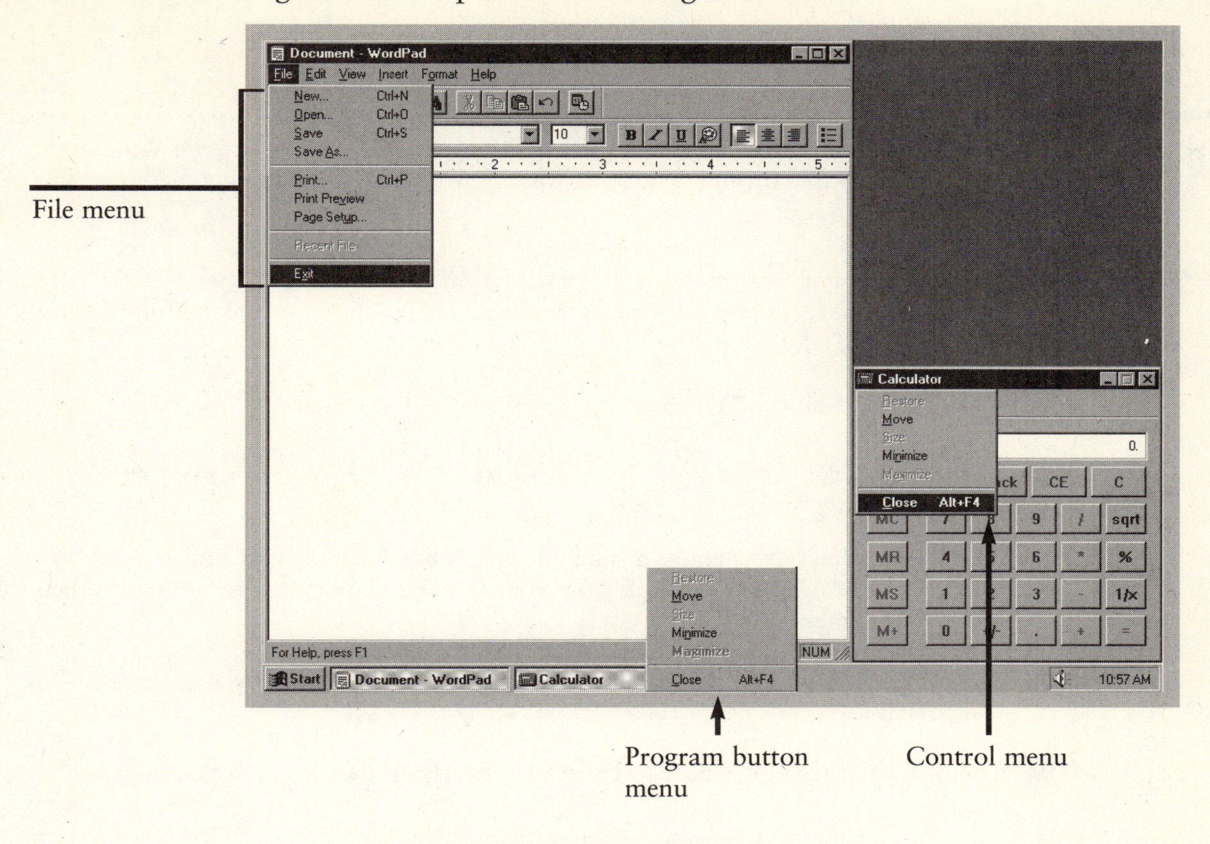

Figure 1-14 Save As dialog box

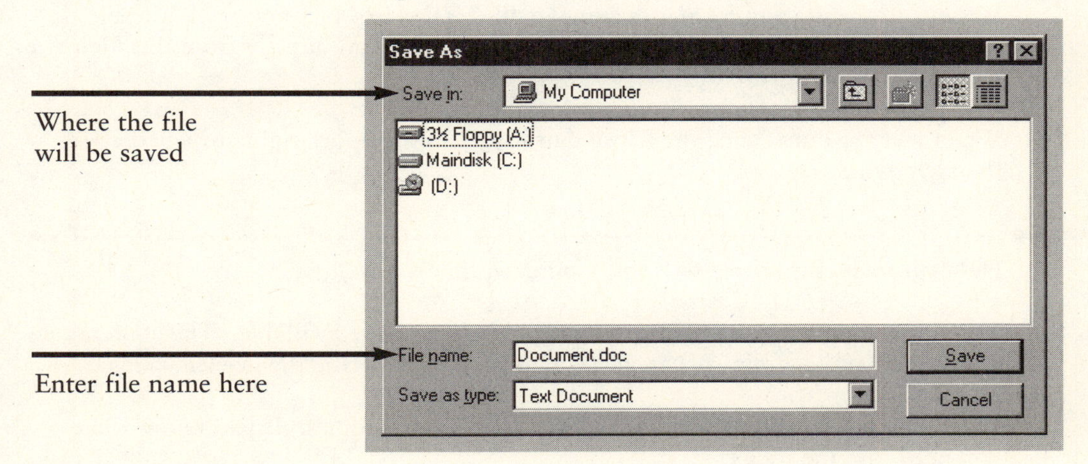

Practice

Open the Calculator and then click the Minimize button. Open the Calculator from the Taskbar. Close the application using the right-clicking method.

Hot Tip

Some applications let you close all open files at once. Press the [Shift] key when clicking on the File menu to change the Close command to Close All.

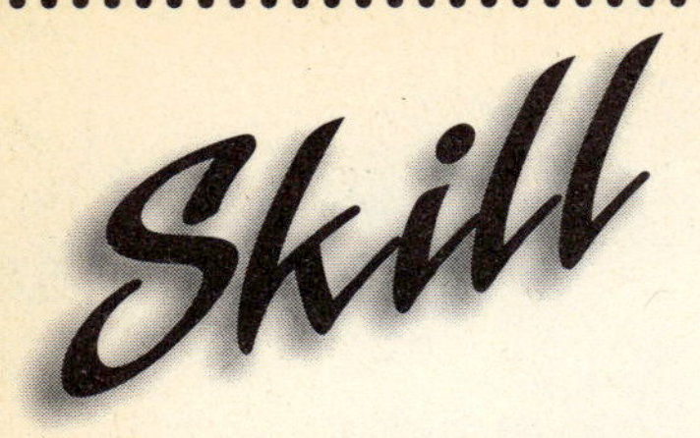

Getting Help

Concept

You might find that you need a little help along the way as you explore Windows 95. The **Help** files include a tutorial, tips and tricks, troubleshooting methods, and a searchable index.

Do It!

Mike wants to learn about the Help facilities. He practices by looking for information on WordPad.

1. Click the **Start** button [Start].
2. Highlight Help and click it. The Help Topics dialog box (as shown in Figure 1-15) will appear.
3. The Help dialog box contains a stack of three tabs. Each of these tabs has a label with a title that describes the tab's function. Click the **Index** tab to bring it to the front of the stack.
4. Type **WordPad** in the blank field above the Index list. As you type each letter, notice that the Index will scroll.
5. Double-click the main WordPad entry, or press the [**Enter**] key, to open the Help file.
6. Click the **Display** command button [Display] to open the Accessories: Using WordPad to write and format documents file. The Help box gives you a brief description of the program. You can even start WordPad directly from this Help window.
7. When you are done, click the **Close** button [X] in the upper right corner to close the Help window.

More

Help is broken into three sections: Contents, Index, and Find.

The Contents tab lists categories of general help that are available. The contents are layered and contain subcategories that get more specific the deeper you go.

The Index tab is useful for information about specific topics. If you know what you need, use the Index.

The Find tab allows you to search for specific words or phrases located in Help using key words.

Figure 1-15 Help Topics dialog box

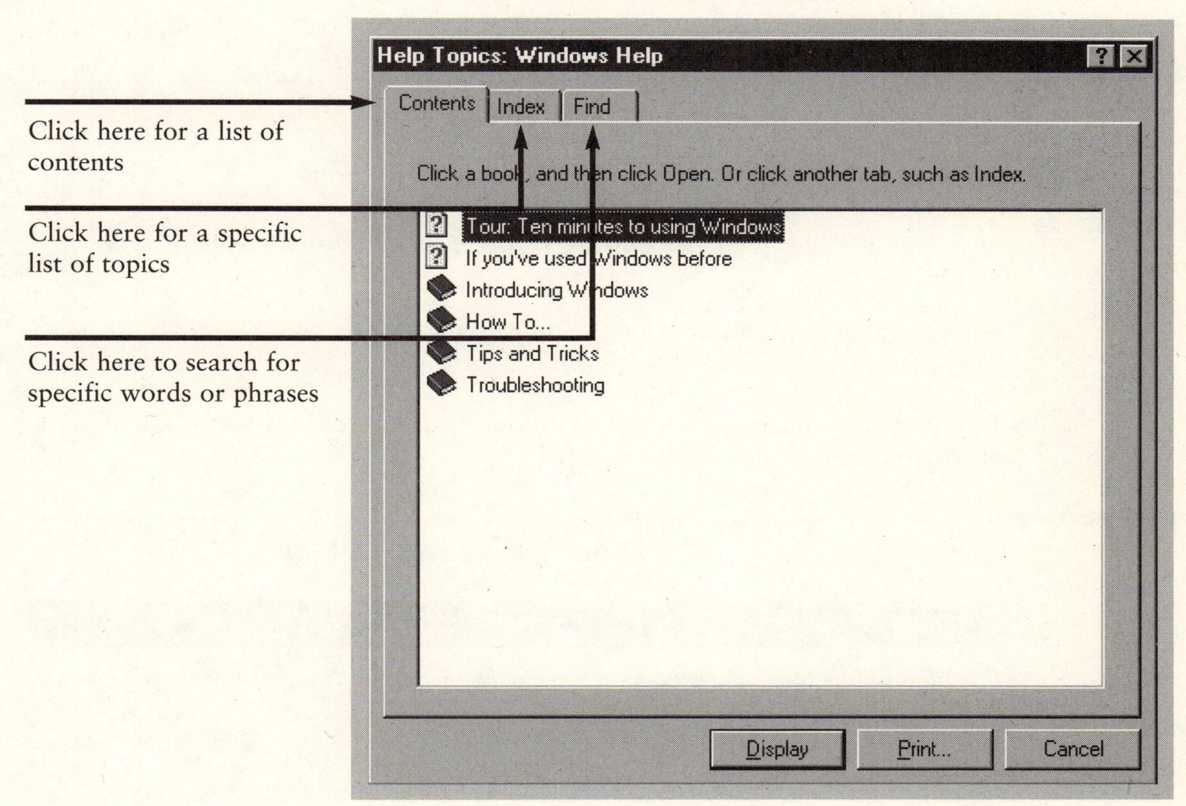

Practice

Look up "help" on the Index tab to display tips for using the function. Close the Help dialog box when you are finished.

Hot Tip

Many dialog boxes have their own Help boxes. Clicking the Help button [?] will change the pointer to one with a question mark. Use this pointer to click the feature that you would like information about.

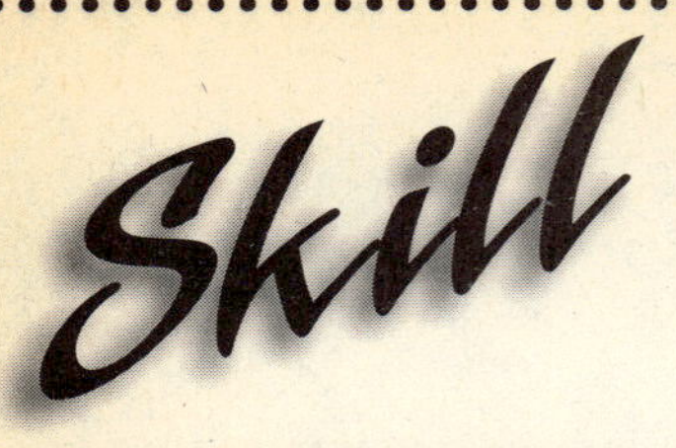

Shutting Down Windows 95

Concept

It is important to **shut down** Windows 95 properly. Failure to do so can result in loss of any unsaved data. When you go through the shut down procedure, Windows 95 checks all open files to see if any unsaved files exist. If any are found, you will be given the opportunity to save them.

Do It!

Mike is ready to shut down and turn off his computer.

1. Click the **Start** button to bring up the Start menu.
2. Click **Shut Down.** A dialog box (Figure 1-16) will appear in the center of your screen.
3. Select the **Shut down the computer** radio button and then click **Yes** to tell Windows 95 that you are ready to end your session.
4. Turn off your computer when you see the message that reads: It's now safe to turn off your computer. (See Figure 1-17.)

More

Shut Down Dialog Box Options

shut down options	result
Shut down the computer?	Prepares the computer to be turned off
Restart the computer?	Restarts the computer and Windows 95
Restart the computer in MS-DOS mode?	Restarts the computer in MS-DOS mode
Close all programs and log on as a different user?	Closes all programs and allows you to log onto Windows 95 with a different name (to use different settings or connect to a network under a different name)

Figure 1-16 Shut Down Windows dialog box

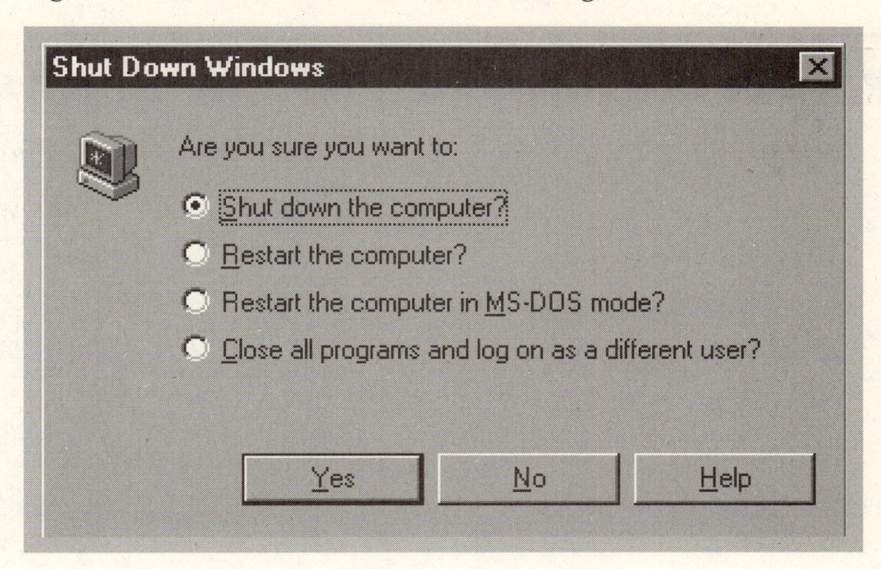

Figure 1-17 Shut Down screen

Practice

Turn on your computer and then restart using the Shut Down dialog box.

Hot Tip

When you are finished using MS-DOS mode, type **exit** or **win** to return to Windows.

Shortcuts

Function	Button/Mouse	Menu	Keyboard
Maximize		Click the Control menu, then Maximize	[Alt] + [F10]
Minimize		Click the Control menu, then Minimize	
Restore		Click the Control menu, then Restore	
Close		Click the Control menu, then Close	[Alt] + [F4]
Move a window	Drag title bar to a new location		
Resize a window	Drag window's border to a new size		
Save a file		Click File, then Save	[Control] + [S]

Identify Key Features

Figure 1-18

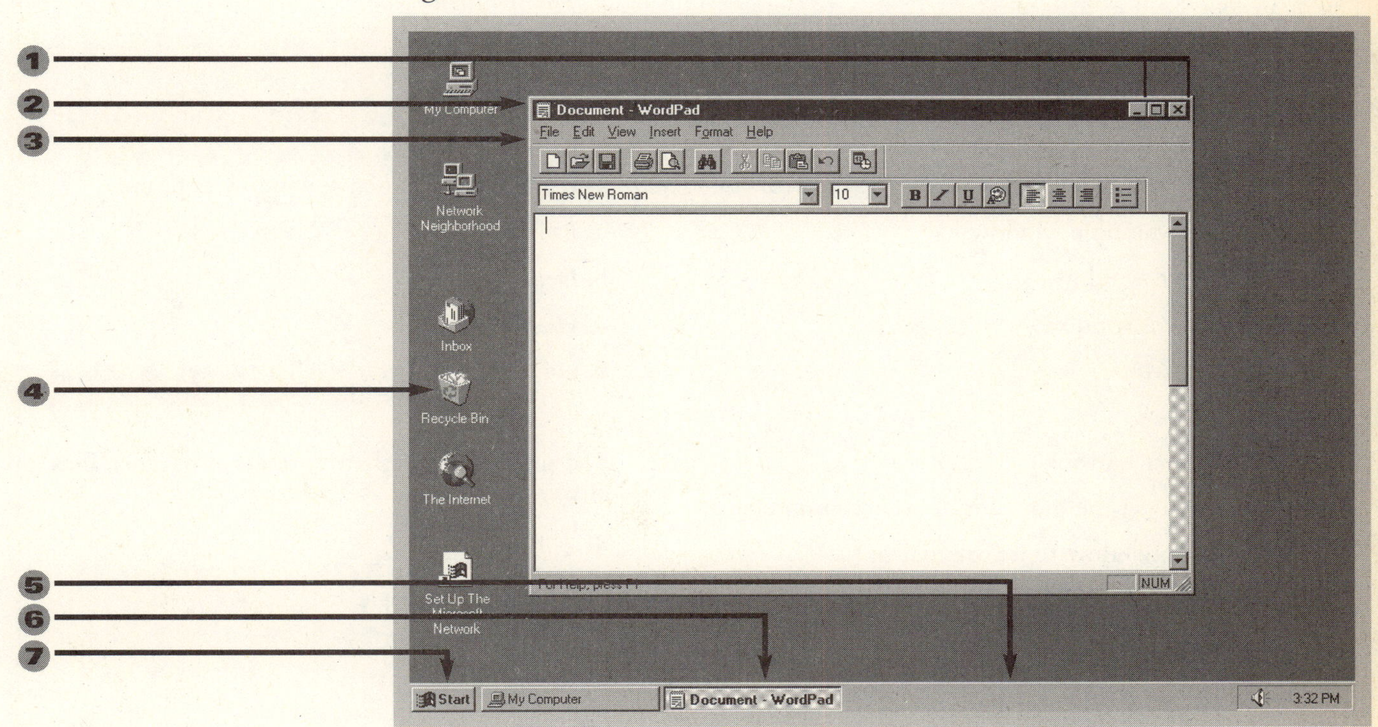

Select the Best Answer

8. A feature that allows you to quickly find files and folders
9. Used to move the pointer across the screen
10. Used to change a window to its original size
11. A shortcut to pop-up menus
12. Where program buttons appear
13. Requests that additional information be given before a command is carried out

a. Taskbar
b. Dialog box
c. Find
d. Right-clicking
e. Restore button
f. Mouse

Quiz (continued)

Complete the Statement

14. You can move an icon by:
    a. Double-clicking the icon
    b. Dragging the icon
    c. Using the arrow keys
    d. Shaking the monitor

15. Right-click on a blank space on the Taskbar to:
    a. Organize multiple windows
    b. Shut down windows
    c. Maximize a window
    d. Open an icon

16. The Maximize button:
    a. Helps you get the most out of your computer
    b. Returns a window to its original size
    c. Expands a window so it fills the entire screen
    d. Shrinks a window to a program button on the Taskbar

17. A menu contains:
    a. Dialog boxes
    b. Tabs
    c. Commands
    d. ToolTips

18. A Radio button:
    a. Is a round button used to select a dialog box option
    b. Plays music when clicked
    c. Appears on all menus
    d. Indicates a dialog box will open

19. The Shut Down command is located on:
    a. The control menu
    b. The file menu
    c. The title bar
    d. The Start menu

20. The title bar of an active window appears:
    a. Raised
    b. Depressed
    c. Highlighted
    d. Dimmed

21. The small pictures that represent programs, files, or drives are called:
    a. Windows
    b. Icons
    c. Buttons
    d. Menus

22. The program button of an active window appears:
    a. Raised
    b. Depressed
    c. Highlighted
    d. Dimmed

23. To move the contents of a window up one screen:
    a. Click once on the up scroll bar arrow
    b. Click once on the down scroll bar arrow
    c. Click once above the scroll bar box in the scroll bar
    d. Click once below the scroll bar box in the scroll bar

Interactivity

Test Your Skills

1. Start Windows 95, identify the items on the screen, and move the icons:
   a. Turn on your computer.
   b. Identify the items that appear on your desktop.
   c. Drag all the icons toward the center of your screen. Be careful not to place them too close together.
   d. Right-click on the desktop and Auto arrange the icons to return them to their original places.

2. Open an icon, resize the window, and then minimize it:
   a. Double-click the My Computer icon.
   b. Double-click the C: drive icon.
   c. Maximize the window.
   d. Click the View by Large Icons button.
   e. Restore the window to its previous size.
   f. Resize the window by dragging the window's borders until you see vertical and horizontal scroll bars.
   g. Use the scroll bars to move the contents of the window down one screen and right one screen.
   h. Minimize the window.

3. Run multiple programs and use menus and dialog boxes:
   a. Click the Start menu, highlight Programs, then Accessories, then click Calculator.
   b. Repeat step a for WordPad and Notepad.
   c. Right-click the Taskbar and select Cascade from the pop-up menu.
   d. Activate WordPad. Type your name and then drag the mouse pointer, an I-beam in this instance, over the text to highlight it.
   e. Click the Format menu and select Font.
   f. Pick a new font and size and then click the OK button.
   g. Select Save As from the File menu and save the document on the desktop under a file name of your choice.

4. Close all open applications and shut down your computer:
   a. Click the control menu in WordPad and select Close.
   b. Click the Notepad File menu and select the Close command.
   c. Click the Calculator and My Computer program buttons from the Taskbar, then click their Close buttons.
   d. Click the Start button and select Shut Down.

Interactivity (continued)

Problem Solving

Using the skills you learned in Lesson 1, set your desktop to look like the one in Figure 1-19. Since many computers have different programs installed, and many settings get changed over time, you may have a slightly different setup and different desktop icons. It is OK if your desktop does not match the figure exactly.

Notice:

1. WordPad program button
2. Toolbar
3. Large icons
4. Rearranged desktop icons

Figure 1-19

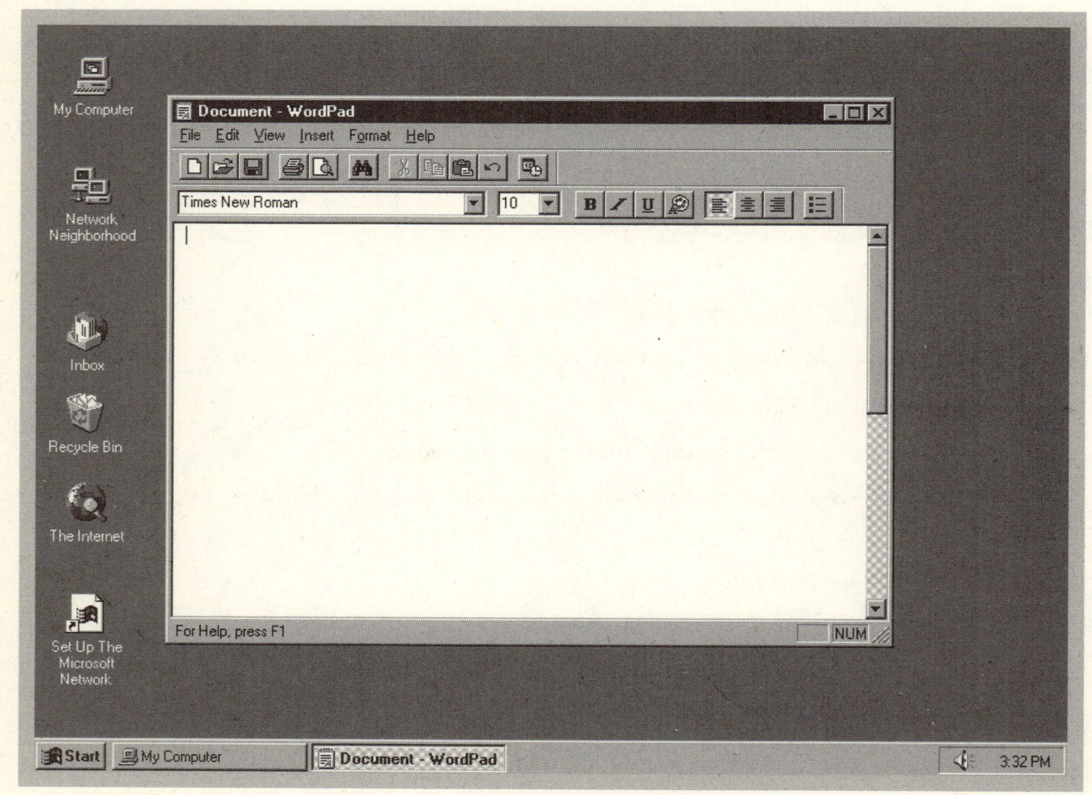

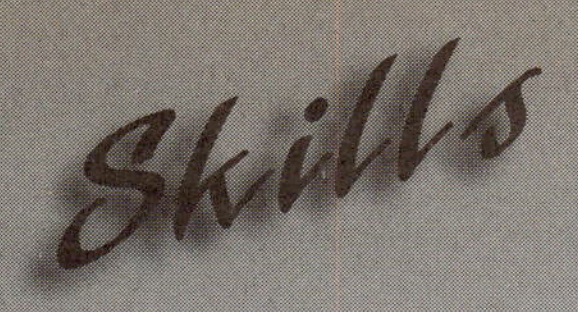

- Examining My Computer
- Examining the Windows Explorer
- Creating Folders
- Moving and Copying Files and Folders
- Building Shortcuts
- Finding Files
- Using the Recycle Bin

LESSON 2

MANAGING FILES

A file is a document, picture, or any other collection of information that is stored under its own unique name. A **folder,** much like a paper folder, is a collection of files that can also house other folders. Your computer stores electronic files and folders as you might store paper ones in a metal filing cabinet. To make finding files and folders easier you should group them in an organized and logical manner. The manner in which your files and folders are arranged is called a **file hierarchy.**

A file hierarchy, as shown in Figure 2-1, is similar to a family tree. The parent, child, and grandchild branches are substituted with folders. A file hierarchy depicts all the drives, applications, folders, and files on your computer. Placing similar files into well-named folders is the best way to create a meaningful file hierarchy. By viewing the higher levels of your file hierarchy, you will be able to get a sense of where files are stored without having to open each particular folder.

My Computer and **Windows Explorer** are both file management tools. File management can be complex and slightly tricky at first. The key to understanding file management is being able to visualize and organize the placement of your files. Having to search through the entire file hierarchy every time you wish to locate an item can become time-consuming and frustrating. Learning how to manage your files effectively, by understanding My Computer and the Windows Explorer, will help you to get the most out of your computer. My Computer and the Windows Explorer are similar in function and in use. After a brief examination of **My Computer** we will concentrate on **Windows Explorer,** the more versatile file organizer.

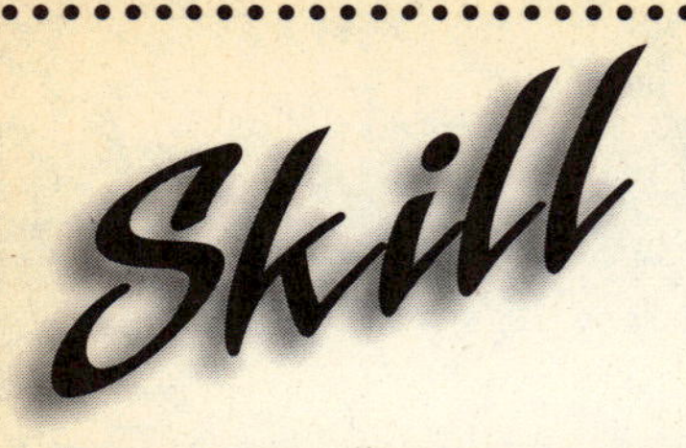

Examining My Computer

Concept

My Computer is a tool that shows you the organization of the drives and configuration folders on your computer. You use My Computer to navigate through the file management of your system. Opening an icon in the My Computer window, usually for a drive or a folder, will show you that particular icon's contents. My Computer allows you to view an item's contents four different ways: by **Large Icons**, by **Small Icons**, in **List** form, or with **Details**. How you view a folder or file will depend on the information you require.

Do It!

To gain a better understanding of file management, Mike wants to explore his C: drive (maindisk) by viewing its contents in the different View forms.

1. Open the **My Computer** window by double-clicking the icon on the desktop with that caption (usually located in the upper left of the screen).

2. To easily toggle between views, you need to make sure your toolbar is visible. Click the **View** menu and guide the pointer onto the **Toolbar** command. If there is no check mark beside Toolbar, click the **left mouse** button.

3. My Computer provides you with two ways to use its windows. You can choose to see a separate window for each open folder, or a single window that changes to match the contents of the folder you have just opened. For this skill you will use the single window. Click **View**, then select **Options**. The Options dialog box will open.

4. If it is not already active, click the radio button that says **Browse folders by using a single window that changes as you open each folder**. Then click the **OK** button at the bottom of the dialog box.

5. The My Computer window (Figure 2-2) displays icons that represent your computer's disk drives and system control folders. Double-click the **C: drive icon** to view the folders on your hard drive.

Figure 2-1 Sample file hierarchy

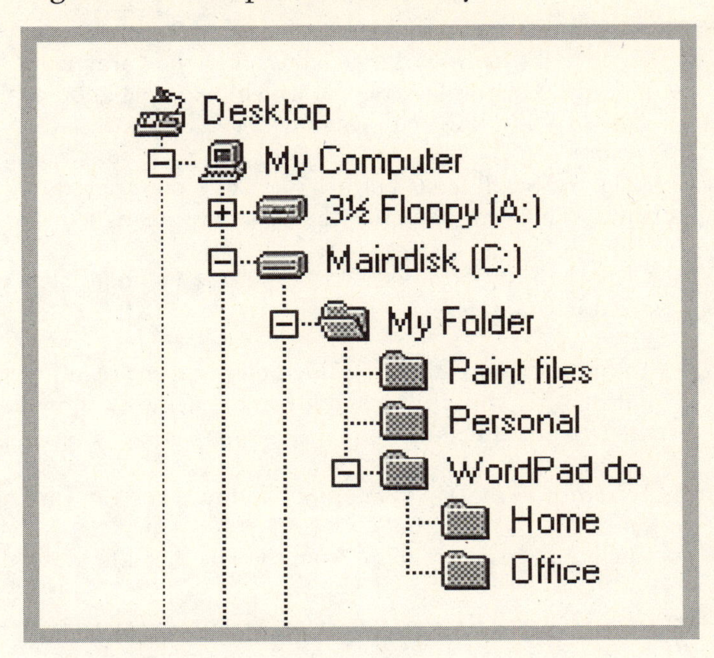

Figure 2-2 My Computer window

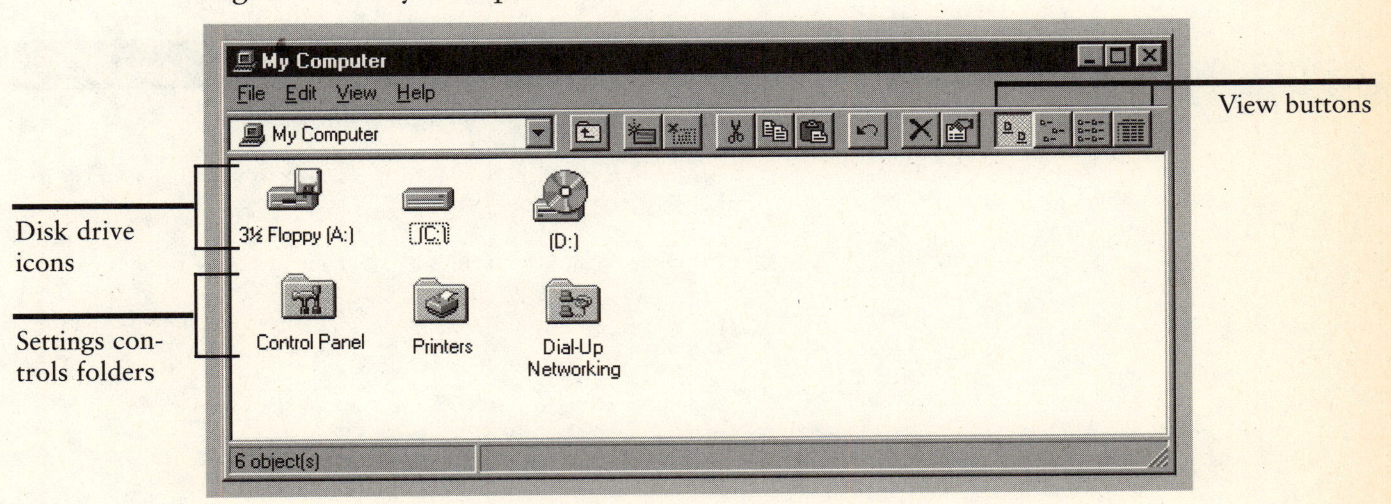

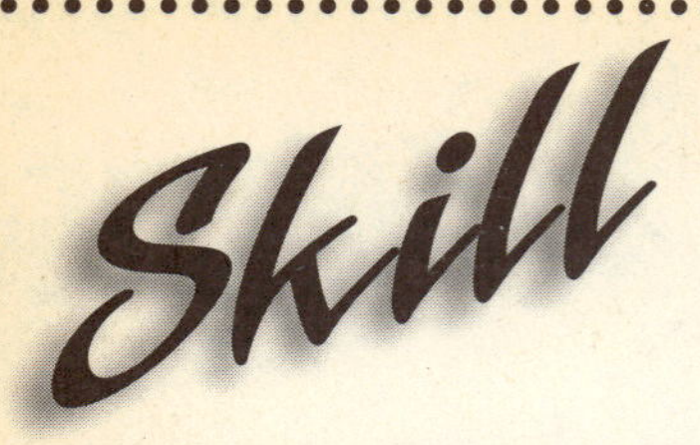

Examining My Computer (continued)

Do It!

6. To view the items by Large Icons, click the **Large Icons** button on the toolbar. Figure 2-3 shows large icons, which take up a good deal of space but offer a clear view of a window's contents.

7. Click the **Small Icons** button. The icons are reduced in size and placed into rows. This view is useful when you have many icons to fit into one window.

8. Click the **List** button. List is similar to Small Icons except that icons are organized in columns.

9. To find out more about a folder, file, or drive than just its name, click the **Details** button. This view will tell you the name of an item, its type, and even the last time you modified it.

10. To return to the My Computer window, click the **Up One Level** button.

11. Click the **Close** command from the **File** menu to close all open windows.

More

Just as you have a choice of how you see an icon, you also can choose how those icons are arranged in a window. The **Arrange Icons** command is found in the **View** menu. You can also call up this menu by right-clicking an empty space in the window.

Arrange Icons Commands

command	use to
By Name	Arrange your folders or files alphabetically
By Type	Arrange your folders or files by type, such as a document or file folder
By Size	Arrange your folders or files by size from largest to smallest
By Date	Arrange your folders or files by the date on which they were last modified
Auto Arrange	Rearrange icons in neat rows or columns if you have moved them

Figure 2-3 Maindisk (C:) window

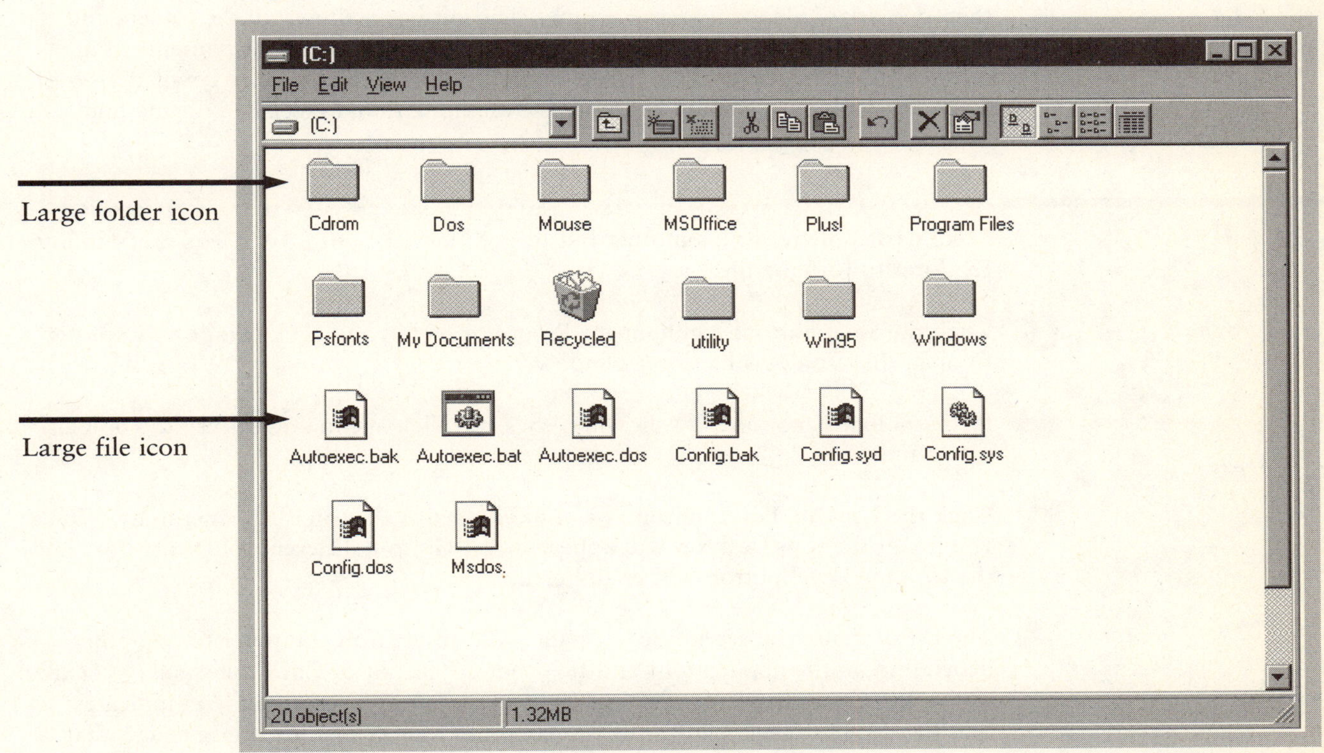

Select the Desktop from the List Box in the My Computer window and rearrange the icons using the option of your choice.

Hot Tip

You can access any icon on your desktop through the List Box [My Computer] on the toolbar.

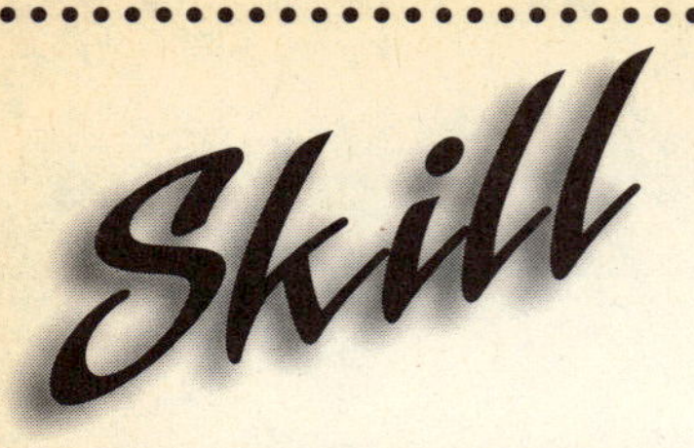

Examining the Windows Explorer

Concept

The **Windows Explorer**, found in the Programs menu on the Start menu, is similar to My Computer. Both are file management tools that allow you to view the contents of your computer. The Windows Explorer is more powerful and provides you with more options than My Computer. The Windows Explorer displays itself as the two-paneled window you see in Figure 2-4, allowing you to work with more than one drive, file, or folder at a time. The left panel shows all the folders and disk drives on your computer. The right panel is a display of the contents of a selected folder or drive. This two-paneled window creates a more detailed view of a specific folder and makes for easier file manipulation, especially copying and moving.

Do It!

Mike wrote a letter to his mother but forgot where he put it. He uses the Windows Explorer to find the file.

1. Click the **Start** button, highlight the **Programs** menu, and click **Windows Explorer** to open the Windows Explorer window.
2. If the toolbar is not already showing, click the **View** menu and select the **Toolbar** command.
3. Click the **Up One Level** button until you get to the top of the hierarchy. When you are at the top, **Desktop** will appear in the **Go to a different folder** list box, and the Up One Level button will be dimmed.
4. The list of items you see in the left panel will differ from computer to computer depending on the applications and files that are installed. Click the small + next to the My Computer icon to reveal its contents. A + next to an icon indicates that the item can be expanded to display other folders that are contained in that drive or folder. There will be no + if the folder only contains files. Expanding an icon reveals another level of the hierarchy. (Clicking the − collapses a drive or folder's contents back into the parent drive or folder.) The folder in the left, All Folders, panel, which is selected, appears opened.
5. Ask your professor where the student files are located. If they are on a student disk, insert that floppy disk into your computer's (A:) disk drive.
6. Click the + for the 3½ **Floppy** drive icon, or click the icon for the drive where the student files are located if they are already stored on your computer or over a network. The folder named Mike's Folder will be shown under the icon for the disk where your student files are stored.
7. Click the + next to **Mike's Folder** to expand it. Then click the folder titled **Personal.** The contents of the Personal folder will be displayed in the right panel.
8. To see what is in the **Letters** folder, double-click the folder's icon. **Letter to Mom** and **Letter to Amanda** are here.
9. Close the Windows Explorer by pressing the [**Alt**] and [**F4**] keys.

More

Explanation of the Toolbar Buttons

button	use to	button	use to
My Computer	Open a different folder or drive menu		Cancel the last action
	Move up one level of the hierarchy		Send a file or folder to the Recycle Bin
	Gray out a file or folder and place it on the clipboard		View the specific attributes of a file or folder
	Duplicate a file or folder and place it on the clipboard		Assign a drive letter to a computer that is on the network (this icon appears only if you are connected to a network)
	Paste a cut or copied file or folder from the clipboard		Removes a networked drive from your system

Figure 2-4 Windows Explorer

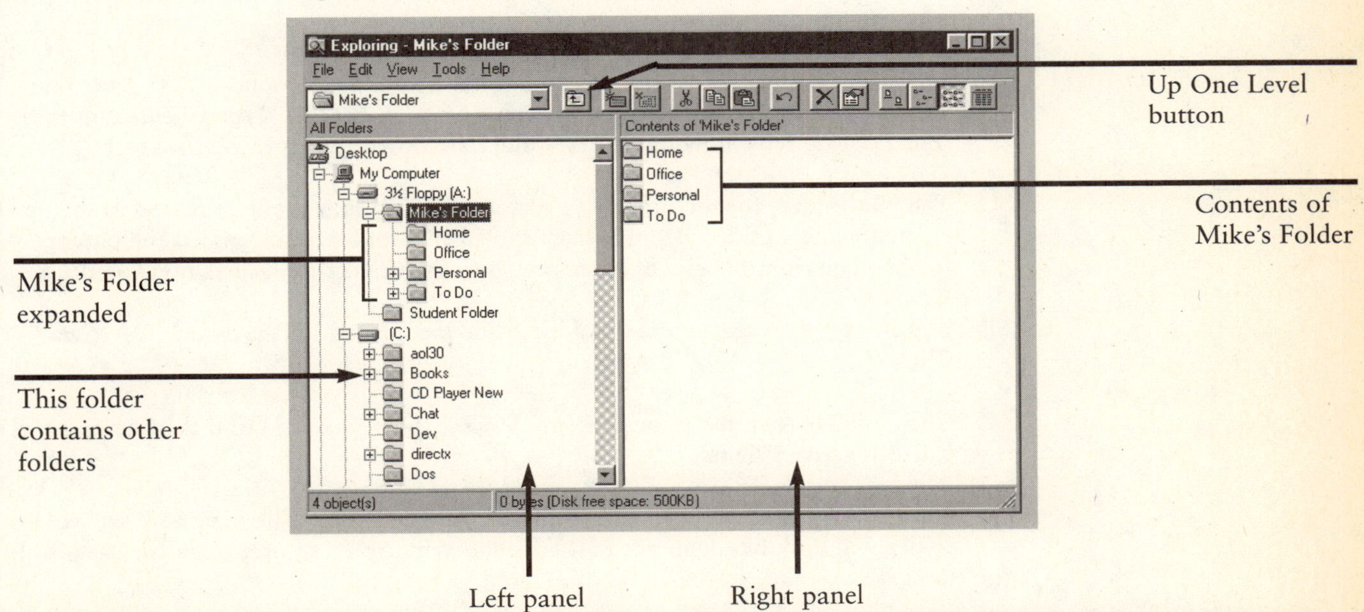

Practice

Click various folders in the left panel to view the contents of your computer, expanding those folders that contain multiple files.

Hot Tip

You can resize the panels of the Windows Explorer. Place the pointer on the bar that divides the window (it will change to ⇹). Drag to the left or right to resize.

Creating Folders

Concept

Creating folders is necessary when you want to store files that are used together in a single location. Creating, naming, and placing folders properly in your hierarchy makes for ease of use and makes your work more efficient.

Do It!

Mike wants to create a folder that will hold the files he has for each of his clients. Within that folder he will need two more folders since his client files are divided into two groups: active and inactive.

1. Open the **Windows Explorer**, insert your student disk into the A: drive, and click the ⊞ next to the 3½ Floppy icon. Or click the drive where your student files are located if they are already stored on your computer or over a network. **Mike's Folder** will appear in the left panel of the Windows Explorer.
2. Click the ⊞ next to Mike's Folder to expand the folder and reveal the other folders nested in it.
3. The parent folder for the new folders will be the one labeled Office. Select the Office folder by clicking it. The right panel will be blank to reflect the fact that the Office folder is empty.
4. Click the **File** menu, point to **New,** then click **Folder**. A folder named New Folder is created in the right panel.
5. The folder name New Folder is highlighted with a box around it indicating that you can replace the selected text by simply typing over it. Type **Clients** and press **[Enter]**. You have now named the folder as shown in Figure 2-5.
6. The two folders for the different categories of customers will be nested in the newly created Clients folder. Double-click the **Clients** folder to select it as the parent folder. The right panel will be empty since the Clients folder has no contents.
7. Repeat step 4 to create a new folder inside the Clients folder. Name it **Active Clients**.
8. Click anywhere in the right panel to deselect the new folder, and then make another called **Inactive Clients**.
9. Click the ⊞ next to the Clients folder in the left panel. The hierarchy for Mike's folder will look like Figure 2-6. Leave the Windows Explorer open for use in the next skill.

More

New folders can also be made by right-clicking. Once a parent folder is selected, right-click a blank space in the right panel. A pop-up menu with a New command will appear, as shown in Figure 2-7. Using this shortcut menu, you can create a folder just as you would using the File menu.

Figure 2-5 Creating a new folder

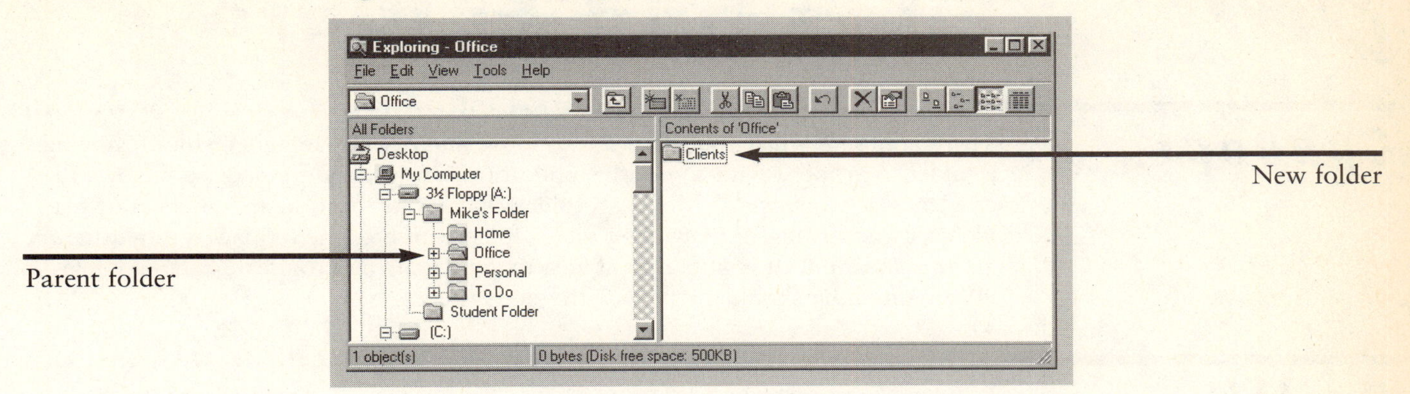

Figure 2-6 File hierarchy with the newly created folders

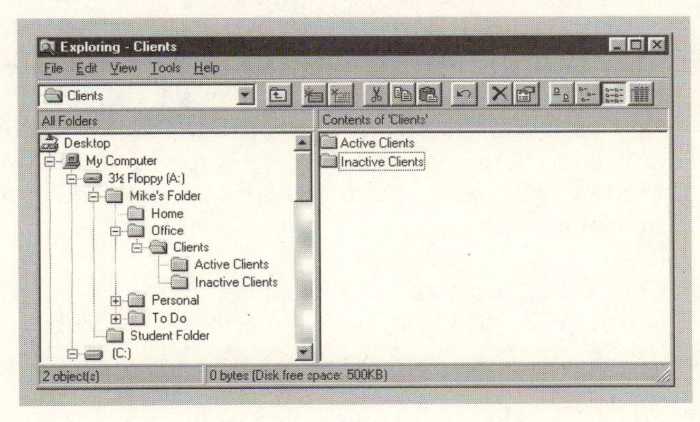

Figure 2-7 Windows Explorer pop-up menu

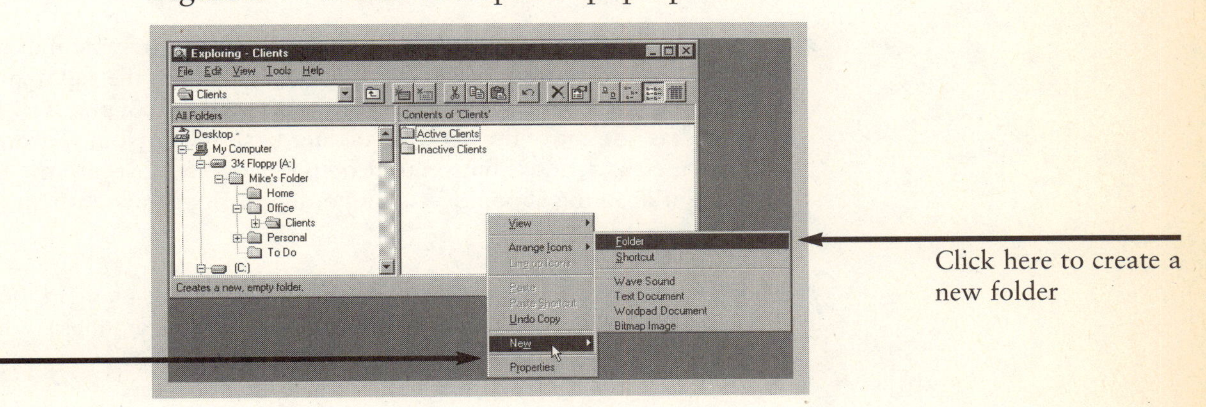

Practice

In the To Do folder, create a new folder named Phone Calls.

Hot Tip

The Rename command allows you to change the name of a folder. Right-click the folder whose name you wish to change, click Rename (or select it, press **[F2]**), type a new title, and press **[Enter]**.

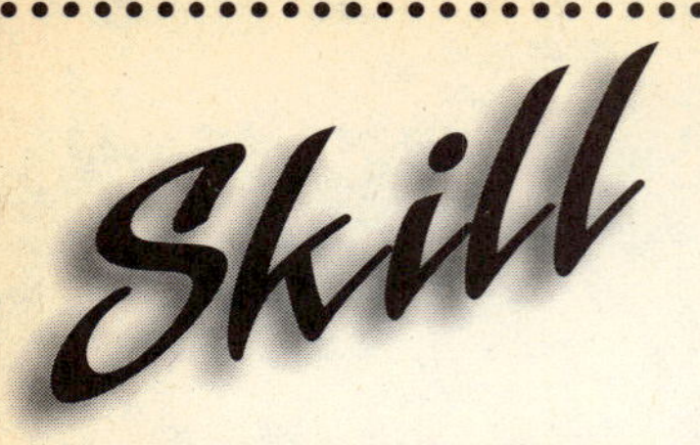

Moving and Copying Files and Folders

Concept

There are times when you will want to **move** and/or **copy** folders or files. Moving a folder to group it with a specific application can be done to increase the overall efficiency of your work. Moving a folder changes its location and alters your file hierarchy accordingly. Copying a file or folder can be done to place a duplicate in another location. It is also a good idea to copy your files to create backup copies in case anything should go awry with your system.

Do It!

Mike wants to move his To Do folder into his Office folder and then make a copy of the Shopping List in his Home folder.

1. Click **Mike's Folder** to list its contents in the right panel.
2. The easiest way to move a folder is by dragging. Drag the **To Do** folder in the right panel to the **Office** folder also in the right panel. You will know that the To Do folder is in the correct position when the Office folder is highlighted, as shown in Figure 2-8. Let go of the mouse button to drop the To Do folder into place. A window will briefly appear showing a page floating from one folder into another, simulating a move.
3. Click the [+] next to the Office folder in the left panel. The To Do folder is now nested inside the Office folder, and the hierarchy has changed to show its new location.
4. You need to locate the **Shopping List** in order to copy it. The Shopping List is housed in the To Do folder. Click the To Do folder icon in the left panel to display its contents in the right panel.
5. Copying can be accomplished in a similar fashion to moving, but you need to use the right mouse button. Drag the Shopping List from the right panel to the **Home** folder in the left panel, using the right button. The Shopping List will appear dimmed as you move it across the divider bar. When Home becomes highlighted, release the right mouse button to drop the Shopping List into the Home folder. After you drop the Shopping List, a pop-up menu, shown in Figure 2-9, will appear.
6. Click **Copy Here**. A copy of the Shopping List will be made in the Home folder. (Notice that you can also move files or folders in this manner.)
7. Click the **Home** folder to see that a copy is indeed there.

More

You can also move and copy with the toolbar buttons. To move, first select the item you wish transported by clicking it. Next, click the **Cut** button to send the file or folder to the Clipboard. Then click a destination folder. Finally, click the **Paste** button to complete the move. Copying is accomplished by using the **Copy** button instead of the Cut button.

Figure 2-8 Moving the To Do folder

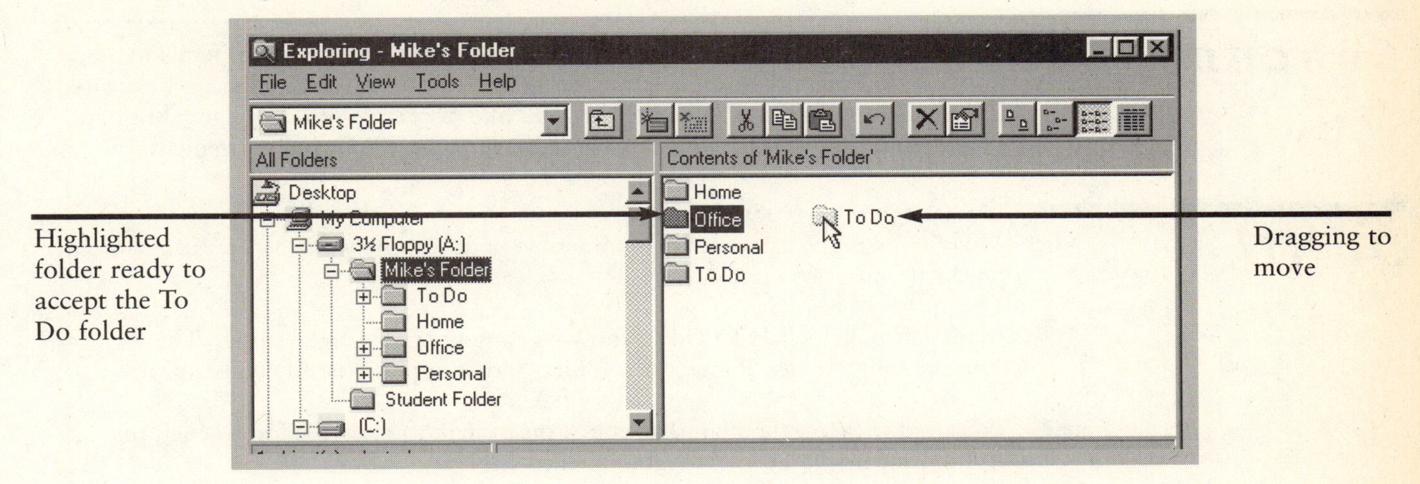

Figure 2-9 Copying the Shopping List

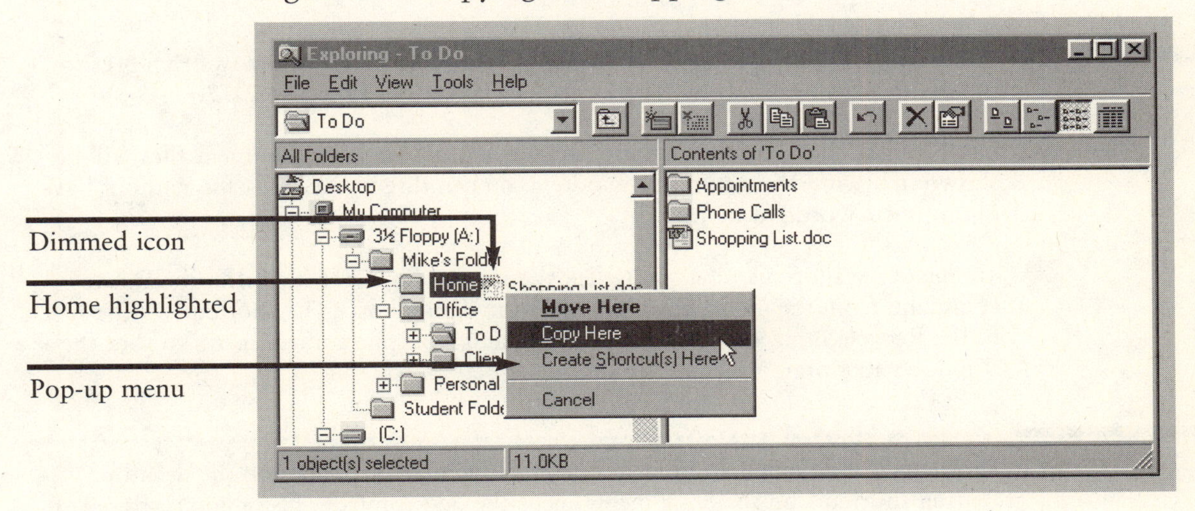

Practice

Copy the letter Mike wrote to his mother from the Letters folder in the Personal folder into his Home folder using the toolbar button method.

Hot Tip

You can Undo a move or copy. This command is found under the Edit menu but is only functional until another command is used.

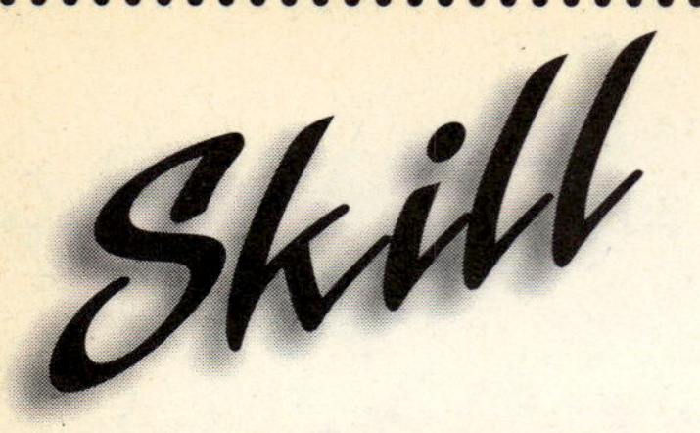

Building Shortcuts

Concept

Shortcuts are icons that give you direct access to a frequently used item so you do not have to open other applications or folders to find it. Shortcuts can be created for a program, folder, file, or even devices like printers. You can place shortcuts directly onto the desktop or Start menu, or anywhere you find convenient.

Do It!

Mike looks in his Appointments folder every day, so he wants to create a shortcut on the desktop for the folder.

1. In the left panel, click **To Do** to show its contents in the right panel. The Appointments folder, Phone Calls folder, and Shopping List file will appear.

2. You need to select the item that you want to make a shortcut for, so click the **Appointments** folder in the right panel to select it.

3. Click **File**, then click **Create Shortcut**. Figure 2-10 shows the new folder created in the right panel named **Shortcut to Appointments**, with a shortcut arrow in the corner.

4. Right-drag the shortcut to an empty space on the desktop. A pop-up menu, as shown in Figure 2-11, will be displayed.

5. Select **Move Here**. The shortcut folder will move from the Windows Explorer to the desktop and will appear as a large icon, as it does in Figure 2-12.

6. Double-click the **Shortcut to Appointments** icon. Mike's appointment files will be shown in a window. From this window you can directly access a file without having to open WordPad first.

7. To delete the shortcut, first right-click the icon to highlight it. Select the **Delete** command from the menu, then **Yes** from the dialog box. The shortcut will be sent to the Recycle Bin. Select the **Close** command from the control menu to shut the Windows Explorer.

More

Shortcuts can be made and put on the Start menu, rather than on the desktop. Putting shortcuts on the Start menu keeps the desktop from becoming cluttered with icons and still offers you quick and direct access to a program, folder, file, printer, etc.

To place an item on the Start menu, you simply drag it from the Windows Explorer to the Start button Start. When you are over the Start button, and the shortcut arrow appears with the dimmed item, then you can drop it. The shortcut will appear on the first level of the Start menu. You will now be able to open the item directly from the Start menu.

Figure 2-10 Shortcut folder

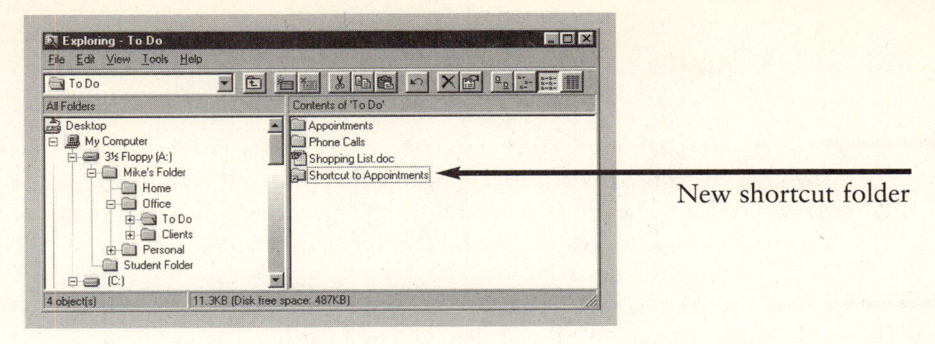

Figure 2-11 Moving a shortcut

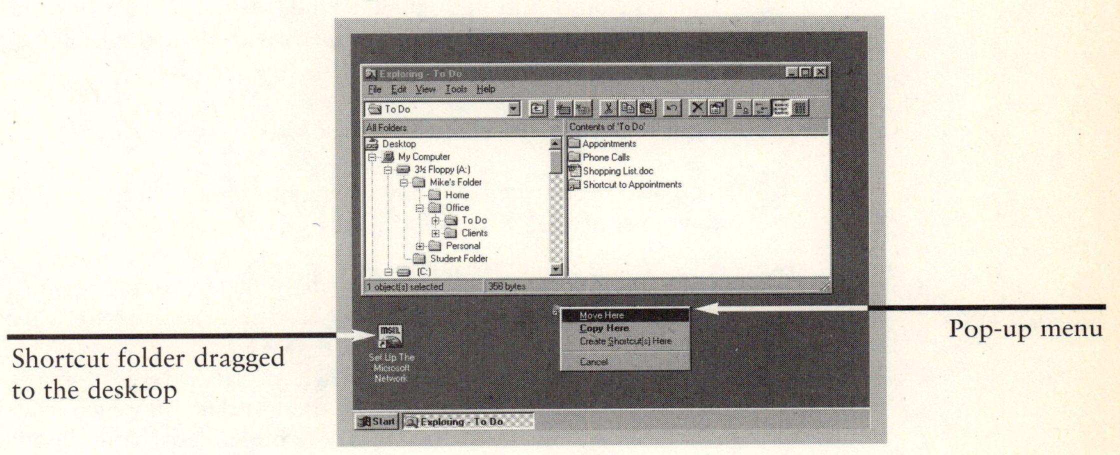

Figure 2-12 Shortcut placed on the desktop

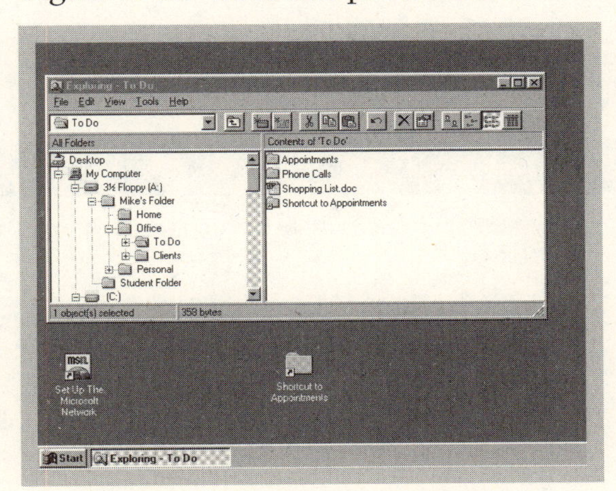

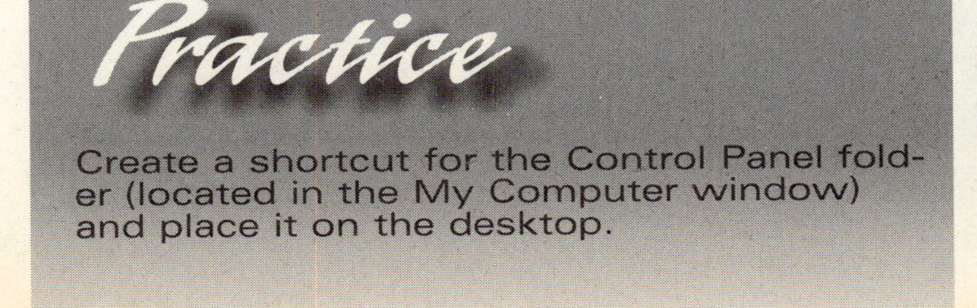

Create a shortcut for the Control Panel folder (located in the My Computer window) and place it on the desktop.

You can create a folder to hold multiple shortcut icons.

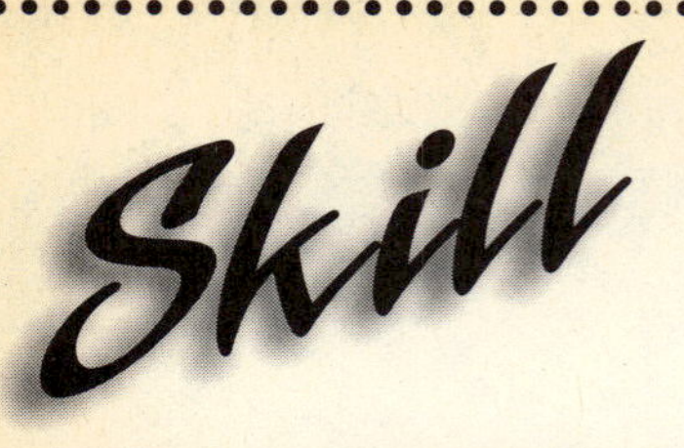

Finding Files

Concept

Managing your files effectively means that you will be able to **find** an item when you need it. The Find command on the Start menu is a tool that searches your computer and locates files or folders for you.

Do It!

Find a letter named Moved, which Mike has created to inform his clients about his recent move.

1. Click the Start button, highlight Find, then click Files or Folders. Figure 2-13 shows the Find dialog box that opens with the default Name & Location tab at the front of the stack.
2. Type Moved in the Named: text box.
3. You also need to tell Windows where to look for the file. Click the Look in: drop-down list arrow. A list of your drives will appear.
4. Select the 3½ Floppy drive, or the drive where your student files are located, and then click Find Now. Windows will search the drive for a file named Moved.
5. When Find locates the file, as shown in Figure 2-14, it will display the full file name, its location, size, type, and the last date on which it was modified. Double-click the Moved file icon to open the file directly from the Find dialog box.
6. Close all open windows using the Close button in the upper-right corner of each window.

More

Three Ways to Search for Files by Using Find

tab	search
Name & Location	By file name and/or drive location, also lets you Browse a directory
Date Modified	For a file that was last changed between certain dates, within a specified period of months or days
Advanced	By the type of file, text it contains, or its size

Figure 2-13 Find dialog box

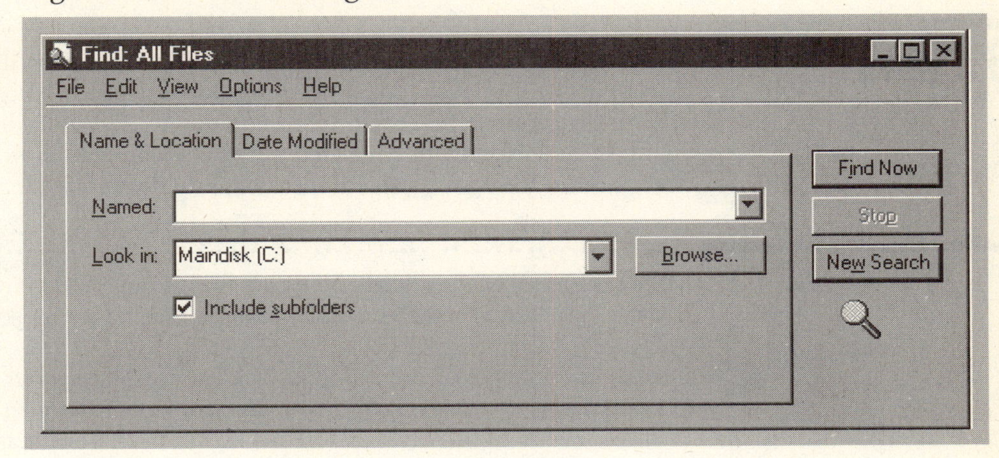

Figure 2-14 A found file

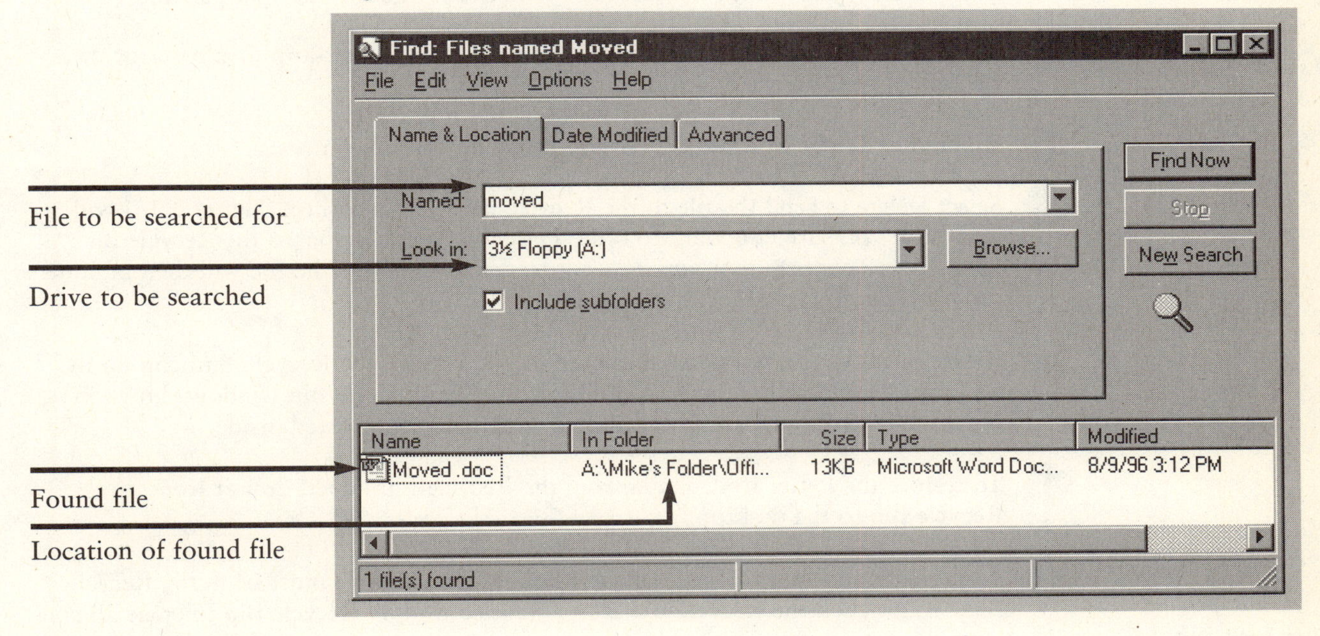

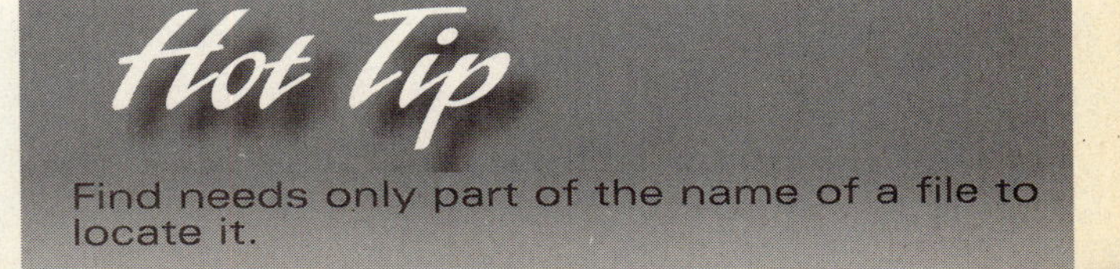

Skill: Using the Recycle Bin

Concept

The **Recycle Bin** is a storage place for files that have been deleted from your hard drive. Files that you no longer need should be deleted in order to save disk space and maximize the efficiency of your computer. If you decide that you need a file again, or have accidentally deleted a file, you can restore it. If you know you will never need a file again, you can permanently delete the file.

Do It!

Mike no longer needs a letter he wrote to Amanda and wants to send it to the Recycle Bin. After he deletes it, he realizes that he wants it back, so he restores it.

1. Files that are deleted from a floppy disk cannot be restored. If your student files are not already on your hard drive, you will have to move the **Letter to Amanda** from your disk to the desktop for this skill. Insert your student disk into the **A: drive** and then open the Windows Explorer from the **Programs** menu.
2. Click the **A: drive** icon or **C: drive** icon, depending on where your student files are, in the left panel of the Explorer, then expand the hierarchy of Mike's Folder by clicking until you see the contents of the Letters folder in the right panel.
3. Drag the **Letter to Amanda** from the right panel to the desktop. An icon for the file will appear on the desktop.
4. Right-click **Letter to Amanda**. A pop-up menu will appear.
5. Select Delete to send the file to the **Recycle Bin**. A dialog box (Figure 2-15) will ask: “Are you sure you want to send ‘Letter to Amanda.doc’ to the Recycle Bin?” Click **Yes** to confirm that you do want to delete the file. The file will then be transferred to the Recycle Bin.
6. Resize or move the Windows Explorer so you can see the Recycle Bin icon on the desktop. Double-click the **Recycle Bin** icon. The Recycle Bin window shown in Figure 2-16 will open and the Letter to Amanda will be listed inside.
7. To restore the Letter to Amanda from the Recycle Bin intact, drag it from the Recycle Bin to the desktop.
8. To permanently remove a file from your computer the file must be in the Recycle Bin. Right-click the **Recycle Bin** icon and select **Empty Recycle Bin** to erase all contents.

More

Various Ways to Delete or Restore a Selected File

to delete	to Restore
Click the Delete button on the toolbar	Click the Undelete button on the toolbar
Right-click and select Delete from the pop-up menu	Right-click the file in the Recycle Bin and select Restore
Drag the file to the Recycle Bin	Drag from the Recycle Bin to any location
Press **[Delete]**	Go to the File menu in the Recycle Bin and select Restore

Figure 2-15 Confirm Delete dialog box

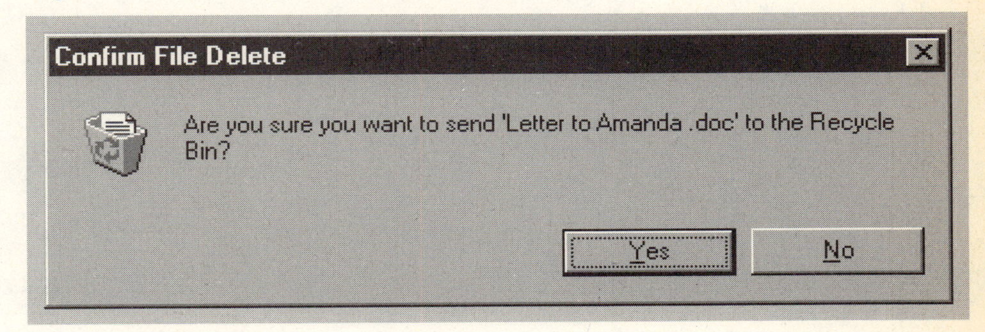

Figure 2-16 Recycle Bin window

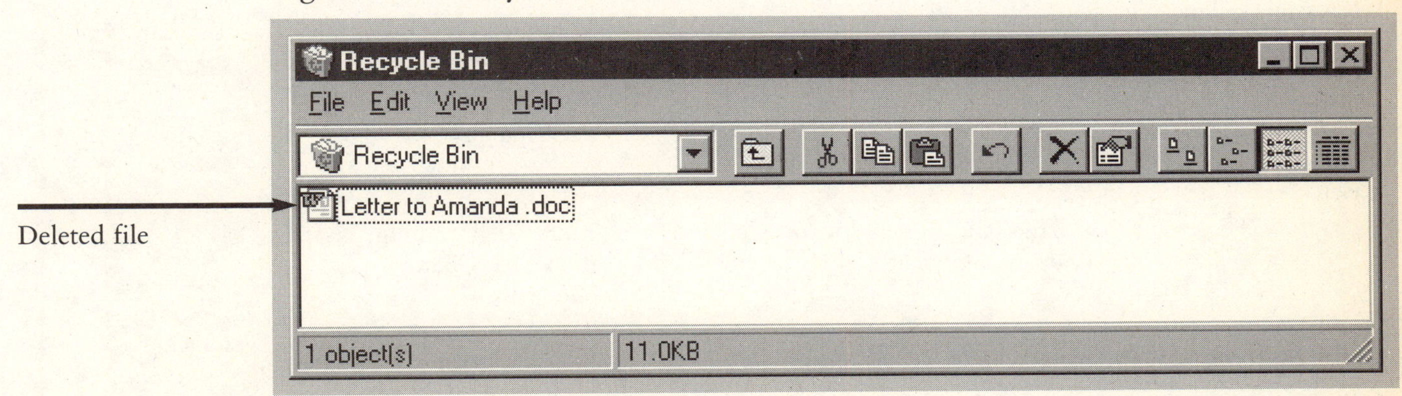

Delete and Restore Mike's folder using the File menu commands.

Files can be erased immediately without being stored in the Recycle Bin. The setting Remove file immediately is found in the Recycle Bin Properties dialog box.

Shortcuts

Function	Button/Mouse	Menu	Keyboard
View files or folders by Large icons		Click View, then Large icons	[Alt] + [V], [G]
View files or folders by Small icons		Click View, then Small icons	[Alt] + [V], [M]
View files or folders in a List		Click View, then List	[Alt] + [V], [L]
View files or folders with Details		Click View, then Details	[Alt] + [V], [D]
Move up one level in the hierarchy			
Cut a file or folder		Click Edit, then Cut	[Alt] + [E], [T]
Copy a file or folder		Click Edit, then Copy	[Alt] + [E], [C]
Paste a file or folder		Click Edit, then Paste	[Alt] + [E], [P]
Undo last action		Click Edit, then Undo	[Alt] + [E], [U]
Delete a file or folder		Right-click, then Delete	[Alt] + [F], [D]
Restore a deleted file or folder	Double-click Recycle Bin, then drag item to new location	Double-click Recycle Bin, right-click on item, then Restore	[Alt] + [F], [E]
Create a new folder		Click File, Highlight New, then click Folder	
Create a shortcut	Drag item to new location, click Create Shortcut Here	Right-click on item, then click Create Shortcut	[Alt] + [F], [S]
Open a different drive	My Computer		

Identify Key Features

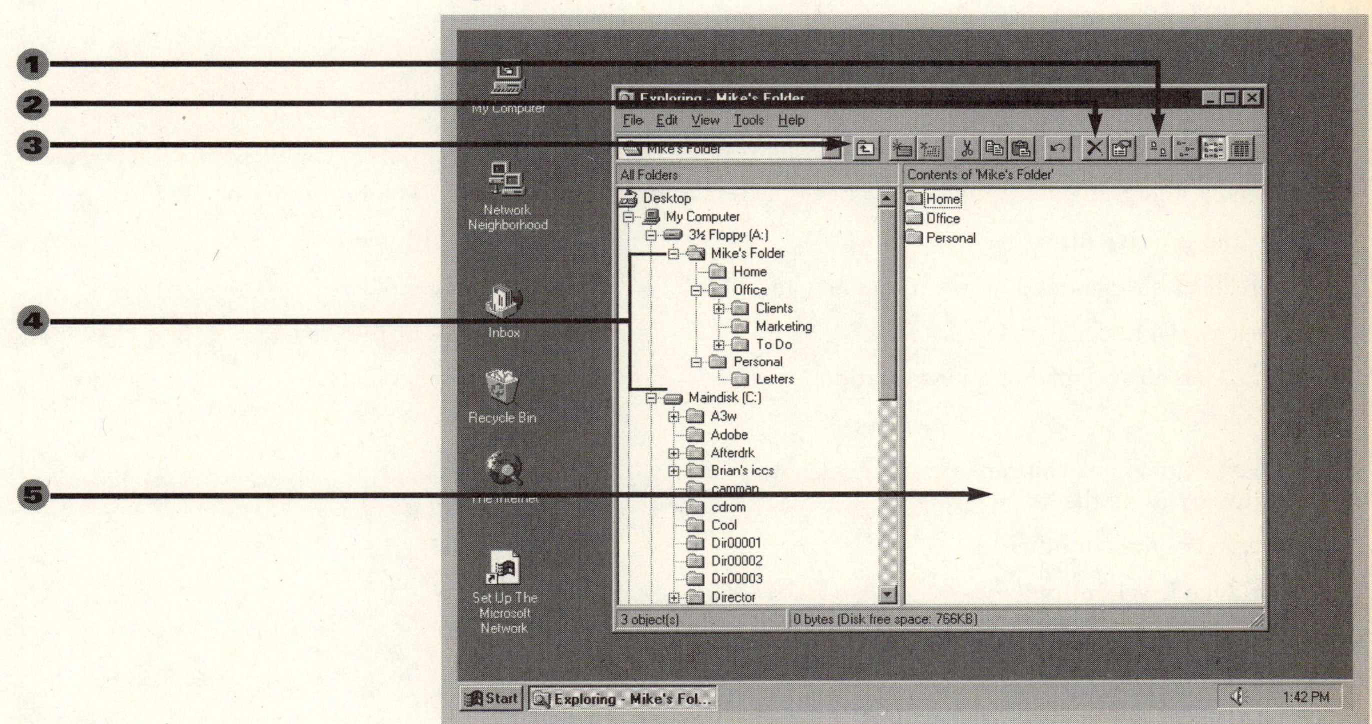

Figure 2-17

Select the Best Answer

6. A unit of information that is stored under its own unique name
7. A tool that shows you the organization of the drives and folders on your computer
8. Command that arranges your folders or files alphabetically
9. An icon that gives you direct access to a frequently used item
10. A storage place for deleted files

a. Recycle Bin
b. Shortcut
c. By name
d. My Computer
e. A file

Quiz (continued)

Complete the Statement

11. To expand a folder in the Windows Explorer so you can view all of its contents, you click the:

    a. Up One Level button

    b. C: drive icon

    c. Plus icon

    d. Minus icon

12. Moving a folder:

    a. Requires heavy lifting

    b. Creates a shortcut and moves it to a new location

    c. Deletes the folder

    d. Transfers the original to a new location

13. With My Computer you can access any icon on your desktop by using the:

    a. List box on the toolbar

    b. Up One Level button

    c. File menu

    d. Control menu

14. The file management tool that allows you view more than one drive, file, or folder at the same time is:

    a. The Windows Explorer

    b. My Computer

    c. Find

    d. The Recycle Bin

15. The Windows Explorer cannot be used to:

    a. Move files or folders

    b. Delete files or folders

    c. Rename files or folders

    d. Resize files or folders

Interactivity

Test Your Skills

1. Open My Computer and View folders:
    a. Double-click on the My Computer icon.
    b. Double-click on the C: drive icon.
    c. Click View, then select Large Icons.
    d. Click the List button.
    e. Right-click in the window, highlight View, and select the Details command.

2. Create two new folders and move one into the other:
    a. Open the Windows Explorer and select the C: drive.
    b. Click the File menu, highlight New, and then select Folder.
    c. Name the folder SPORTS.
    d. Create another folder by right-clicking in the right panel. Name it WRESTLING.
    e. Drag the WRESTLING folder into the SPORTS folder.

3. Create a shortcut for the SPORTS folder:
    a. Right-click the SPORTS folder.
    b. Select Create Shortcut from the pop-up menu.
    c. Drag the shortcut to the desktop.

4. Delete and restore the shortcut to the SPORTS folder:
    a. Click the SPORTS folder on the desktop.
    b. Press the delete key, then click the Yes button from the dialog box.
    c. Open the Recycle Bin.
    d. Select the Shortcut to Sports.
    e. Select Restore from the File menu.
    f. Drag the shortcut on the desktop, and the original Sports folder on the hard drive, to the Recycle Bin.

Interactivity (continued)

Test Your Skills

5. Find the WRESTLING folder:
   a. Click the Start button, highlight Find, and then select Files or Folders.
   b. Type Wrestling.
   c. Click the Find Now button.

Problem Solving

Dovetail, the cabinetmaking shop that you own, is growing by leaps and bounds. You have decided to start organizing your files on your computer. You must create folders for your documents and place some already existing files into these folders.

1. Using the Windows Explorer create folders named Dovetail, Orders, Invoices, and Delivery Dates in the C: drive.
2. Inside the Orders folder create two more folders named Special and Materials.
3. Create two folders inside the Invoices folder named Paid and To Be Paid.
4. Move the Materials, Invoices, and Deliveries folders into the Dovetail folder.
5. Find the files named Order1, Order2, and Delivery from your student disk.
6. Make a copy of the Order1 and Order2 files in the Materials folder and place a copy of the Delivery file into the Deliveries folder.
7. Create a shortcut on the desktop for the Dovetail folder.
8. Delete the Dovetail folder and its shortcut after your instructor views your completed task.

Skills

- Customizing: The Settings Folder
- Customizing: The Mouse
- Customizing: Date and Time
- Customizing: The Display
- Customizing: The Taskbar
- Customizing: The Start Menu
- Loading New Software
- Learning Multimedia

LESSON 3

ADVANCED FUNCTIONS

Windows 95 allows you to customize your environment to suit your personal needs and preferences. You can adjust settings that affect the function and look of the Windows operating system, as well as the settings that affect input devices such as printers and the mouse. The Settings feature on the Start menu has three items that contain the options for altering various properties of the Windows environment.

Most of the Windows features can be adjusted using the Control Panel. The Control Panel window contains a number of icons that represent various elements of Windows 95. The Printers folder permits you to change settings that involve printers. Selecting the Taskbar options opens a dialog box that you use to customize the Taskbar.

In this lesson Mike will be customizing his mouse, the date and time on his computer, the appearance of his display, the Taskbar, and his Start menu. Then he will walk through the steps of loading new software onto his computer. Lastly, he will explore Windows applications that allow you to play and control multimedia.

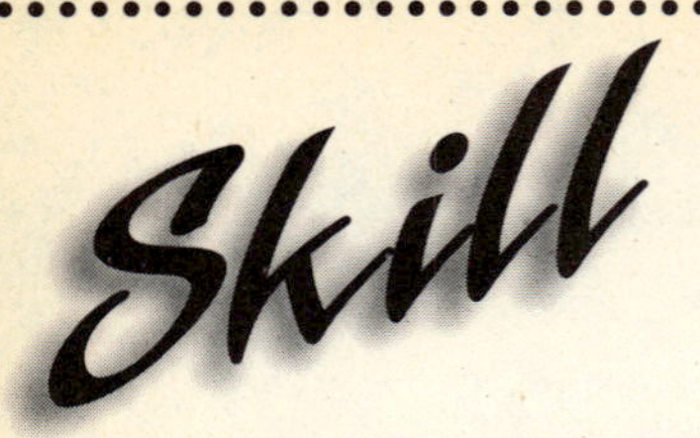

Customizing: The Settings Folder

Concept

The **Settings Folder** is located on the Start menu. It contains folders for the Control Panel and Printers, and an icon for the Taskbar Properties dialog box. Using the icons located in these folders, you can customize certain aspects of your computer to suit your needs.

The Control Panel contains icons that allow you to customize your Windows setup. Through the Control Panel, you can configure your hardware and software, alter the appearance of your desktop, and change the settings of input devices, such as a keyboard and mouse, and various applications. The Printers folder is used to establish which printer you are connected to and it allows you to view the status of a file being printed. The Taskbar dialog window provides you with options for altering the Taskbar and adding or removing Start menu programs.

Do It!

Mike explores the Control Panel, Printers, and Taskbar windows.

1. Click the **Start** button and move the pointer over **Settings** to highlight it. The Settings menu items — Control Panel, Printers, and Taskbar — will pop out, as shown in Figure 3-1.

2. Guide the pointer onto the **Control Panel** folder icon and click to open it. Then click the **Maximize** button so the window fills the entire screen.

3. Right-click on a blank space in the Control Panel window, highlight **View** on the pop-up menu, and select **Large** icons.

4. Put the icons in alphabetical order by right-clicking a blank space in the window, highlighting **Arrange Icons** and selecting **by Name**. Alphabetically arranged icons make for easier viewing. Your window should look like Figure 3-2.

5. Make sure the status bar, the dialog along the bottom of the window, is turned on. Click the **View** menu. If there is a check next to Status Bar ✔ Status Bar, it is active. If not, then click Status Bar.

6. One by one, click each icon in the window. To learn about each icon, read the brief description of the item's function that appears on the status bar.

Figure 3-1 Settings menu

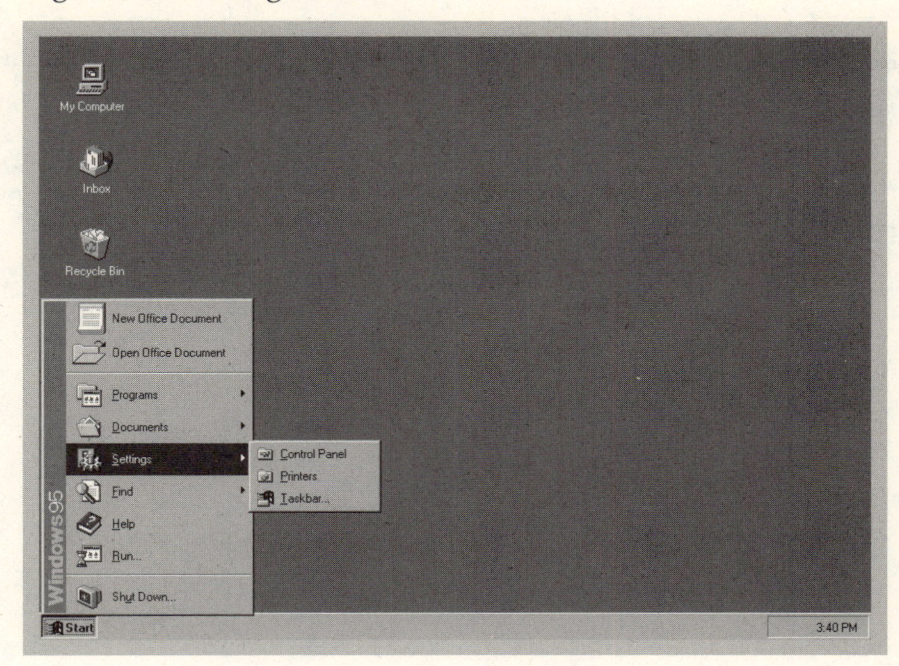

Figure 3-2 Control Panel window with icons arranged alphabetically

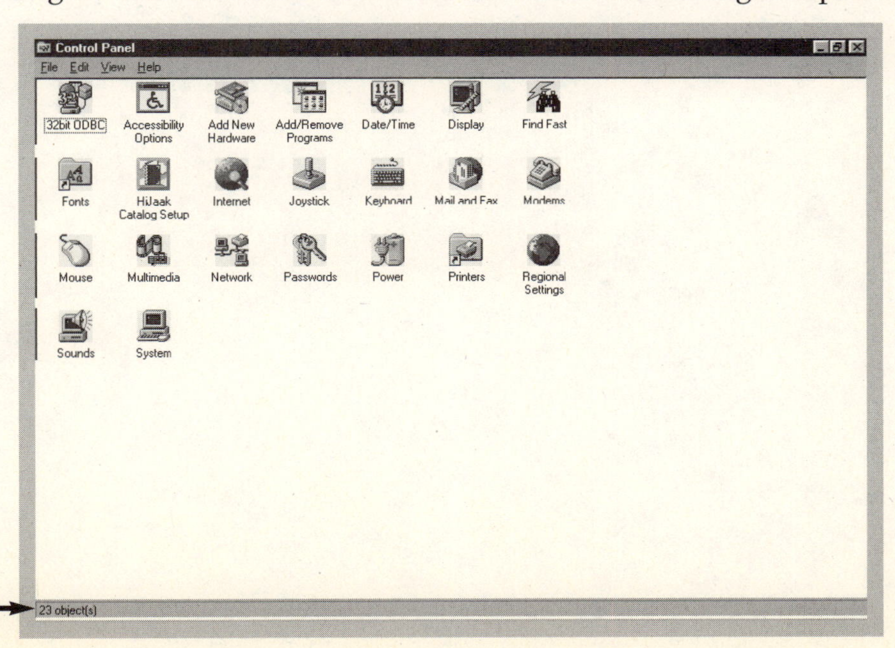

Status bar

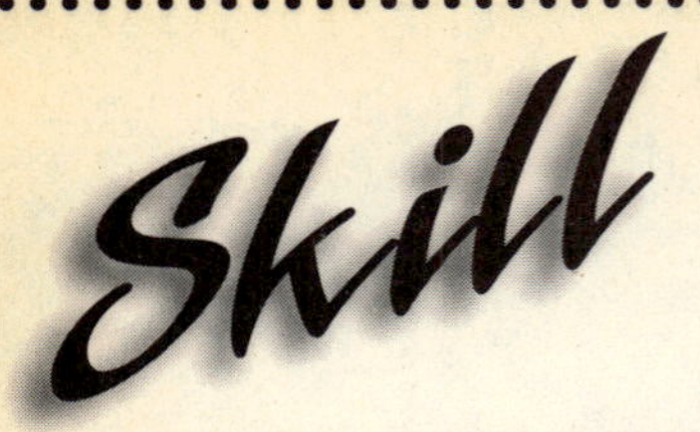

Customizing: The Settings Folder (continued)

Do It!

7. Close the Control Panel window by selecting **Close** from the control menu.

8. Click the **Start** button and open the **Printers** window from the Settings menu. The printers that are connected to your computer will appear as icons in the Printers window, as shown in Figure 3-3. From here you can select the appropriate printer.

9. Double-click any printer in the window to open that printer's window. Click the Printer menu to see the commands available. You can **Pause Printing, Purge Print Jobs, Work Off-line,** or set a **default printer**.

10. Close the two Printers windows.

11. Click the **Start** button and open the **Taskbar Properties** dialog box (Figure 3-4) from the Settings menu. Click each of the tabs to familiarize yourself with the Taskbar control options.

12. Close the Taskbar Properties dialog box by clicking the **Close** button

Figure 3-3 Printers window

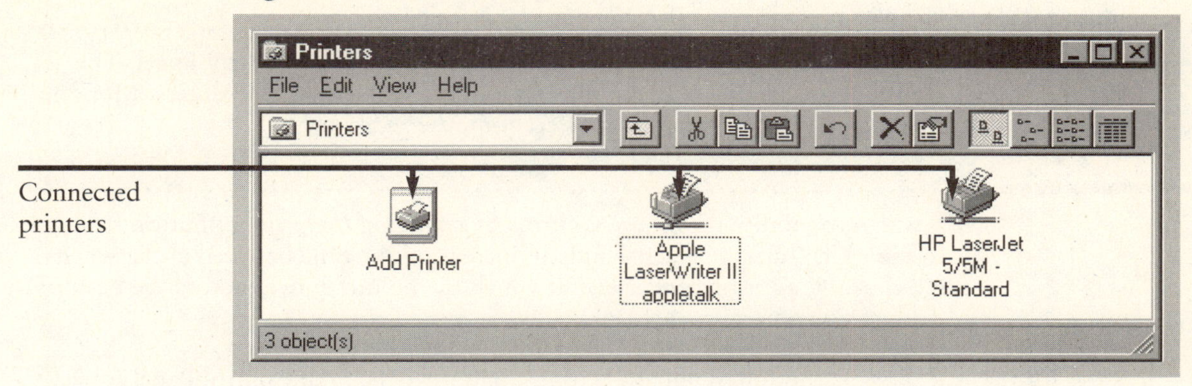

Figure 3-4 Taskbar Properties dialog box

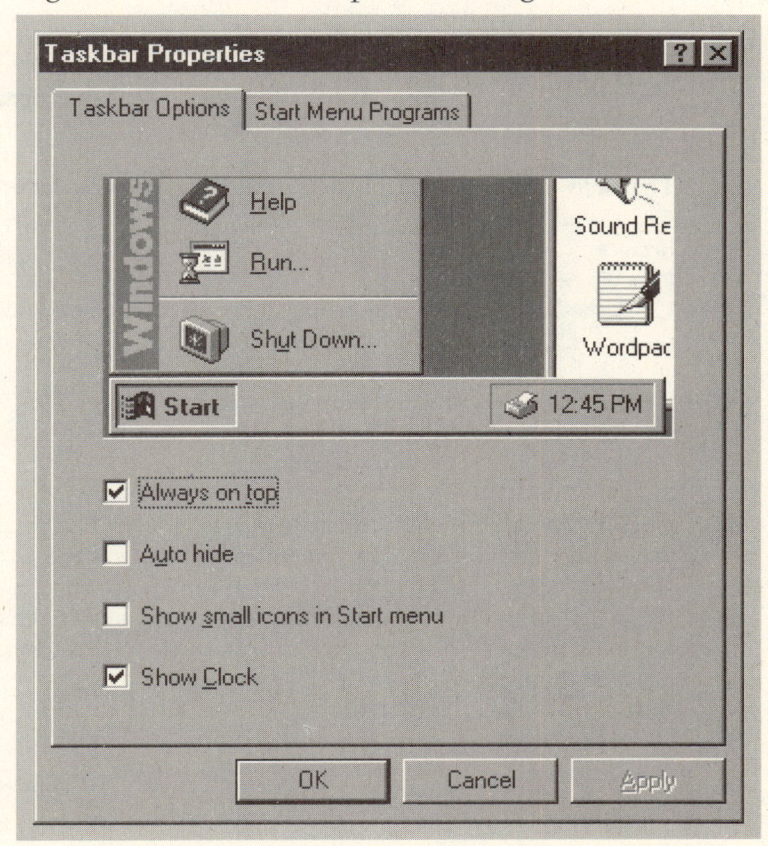

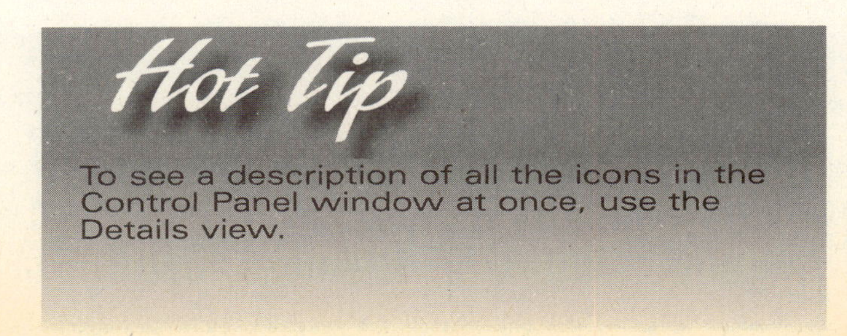

To see a description of all the icons in the Control Panel window at once, use the Details view.

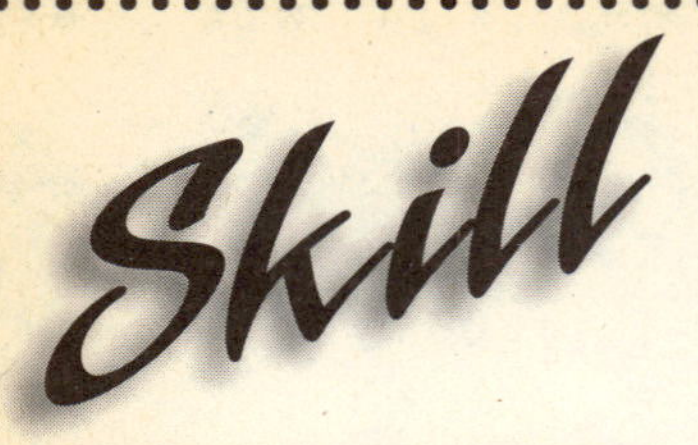

Customizing: The Mouse

Concept

Certain characteristics of **the mouse** can be changed via the Control Panel. The Mouse Properties dialog box contains four file tabs — Buttons, Pointers, Motion, and General — each relating to a different mouse function.

Do It!

Mike wants to modify his mouse controls by changing the primary button from the left to the right (since he is left-handed), increasing the time between clicks when double-clicking, adjusting the speed at which the pointer moves across the desktop, and adding pointer trails.

1. Click the **Start** button, highlight **Settings**, and then click the **Control Panel** folder. After the Control Panel window opens, double-click the **Mouse** icon . The Mouse Properties dialog box (Figure 3-5) will appear with the Buttons tab at the front.

2. Using the **Buttons** tab you can change your mouse's button configuration and double-click speed. Click the **Left-handed** radio button Left-handed to make the right mouse button the primary function button.

3. The slider toward the bottom of the tab controls the time allowed between clicks when double-clicking. Drag the slider to the left to allow a larger amount of time between clicks.

4. Click the **Motion** tab. The controls for **Pointer speed** and **Pointer trails** are found on this tab, as shown in Figure 3-6.

5. Drag the indicator for the Pointer speed to the left. This will adjust the speed at which the pointer moves across the screen in relation to the speed at which the mouse is moved across your desk.

6. Click the check box next to **Show pointer trails**. The shadows the pointer now leaves behind make it easier to spot the pointer on the screen.

7. Click the **Apply** button Apply to save these settings changes. The dialog box will remain open until you click OK or Close. These changes will be undone in the Practice that follows.

8. Close the Mouse Properties dialog box.

More

Description of Mouse Properties Dialog Box Tabs

tab	controls	sets
Buttons	Button configuration Double-click speed	The primary function button The time allowed between clicks of a double-click
Pointers	The appearance of the pointer	The pointer icon displayed during different modes
Motion	Pointer speed Pointer trails	The speed of the pointer relative to the speed at which the mouse is moved The length of the trail the pointer leaves when moved
General	Type of mouse	The type of mouse connected to your computer

Figure 3-5 Mouse Properties dialog box: Buttons tab

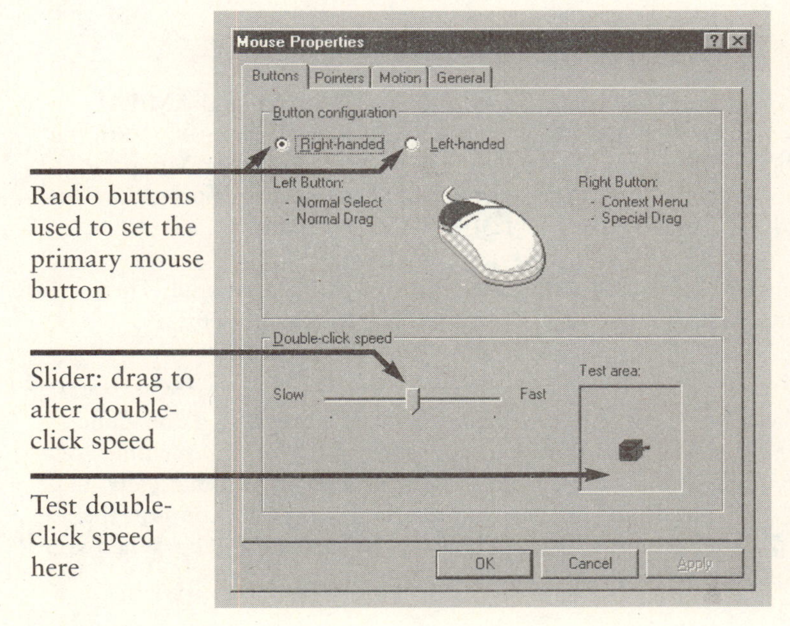

Radio buttons used to set the primary mouse button

Slider: drag to alter double-click speed

Test double-click speed here

Figure 3-6 Mouse Properties dialog box: Motion tab

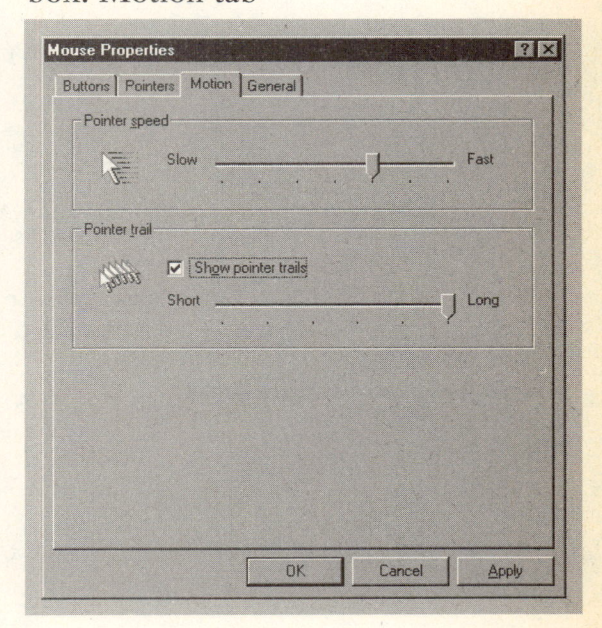

Practice

Reset the mouse for right-handed use, turn off the pointer trails, and set the pointer and double-click speed wherever they are most comfortable.

Hot Tip

Use the Test Area on the Buttons tab to find your preferred double-click speed.

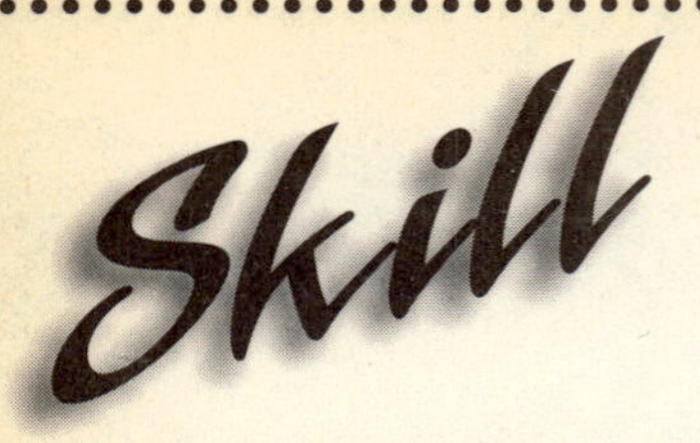

Customizing: Date and Time

Concept

The time of day is displayed on the right side of the Taskbar. If you place the pointer on the clock, the **day, month, date,** and **year** will be displayed in a small pop-up tip box. The icon for the time and date adjustment controls is found in the Control Panel.

Do It!

To see how the Date & Time Property controls work, Mike sets the date and time to 11:30 AM, February 9, 2003.

1. Open the Control Panel and double-click the **Date/Time** icon. Figure 3-7 shows the **Date/Time Properties** dialog box that will appear. The Date & Time tab will be at the front.

2. Click the **months** drop-down box above the calendar to display all twelve months. Select February by moving the pointer to the second month on the list and clicking once. The calendar will change to reflect February's number of days.

3. To change the year, click the **down arrow** button next to the current year until the display reads 2003.

4. Click the **9** on the calendar to set the date.

5. The time box is divided into four parts: hours, minutes, seconds, and AM/PM. Move the pointer over the time text box; it will change to an I-beam I . With the I-beam, click the digit representing the hour to get a blinking cursor. Move the pointer to the arrows and click until the hour reads **11**. Repeat this procedure for the minutes, seconds, and AM/PM until **11:30:00 AM** is displayed.

6. Click Apply to change the time and date to the settings you just entered. Then readjust the time and date to reflect the correct settings for the present.

More

The second tab in the Date/Time Properties dialog box (Figure 3-8), **Time Zone,** allows you to choose the time zone that your computer is set to. If your time zone adjusts for daylight savings time, you can set your computer to automatically make the change. To select a time zone, you can point and click on a location on the map or choose a time zone from the list available at the top of the tab. When you select a time zone, it appears as a lighted band on the map.

Figure 3-7 Date/Time Properties dialog box: Date & Time tab

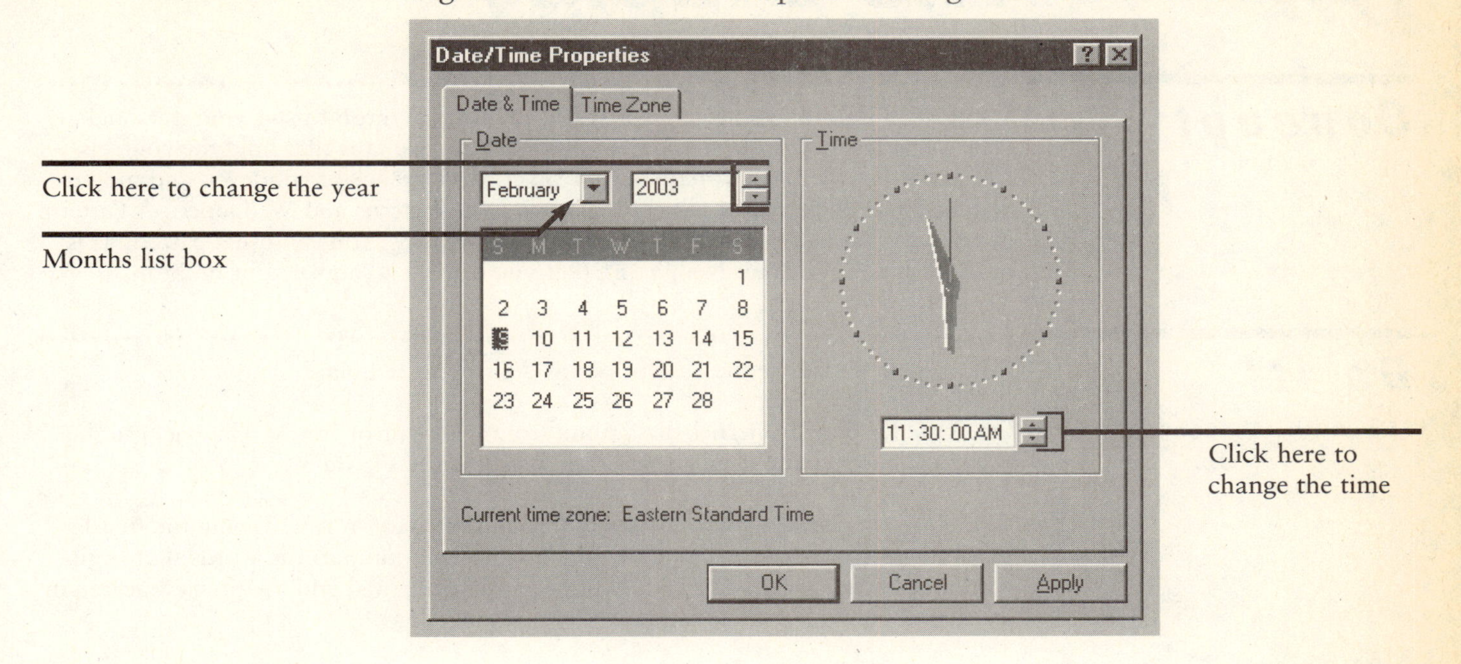

Figure 3-8 Date/Time Properties dialog box: Time Zone tab

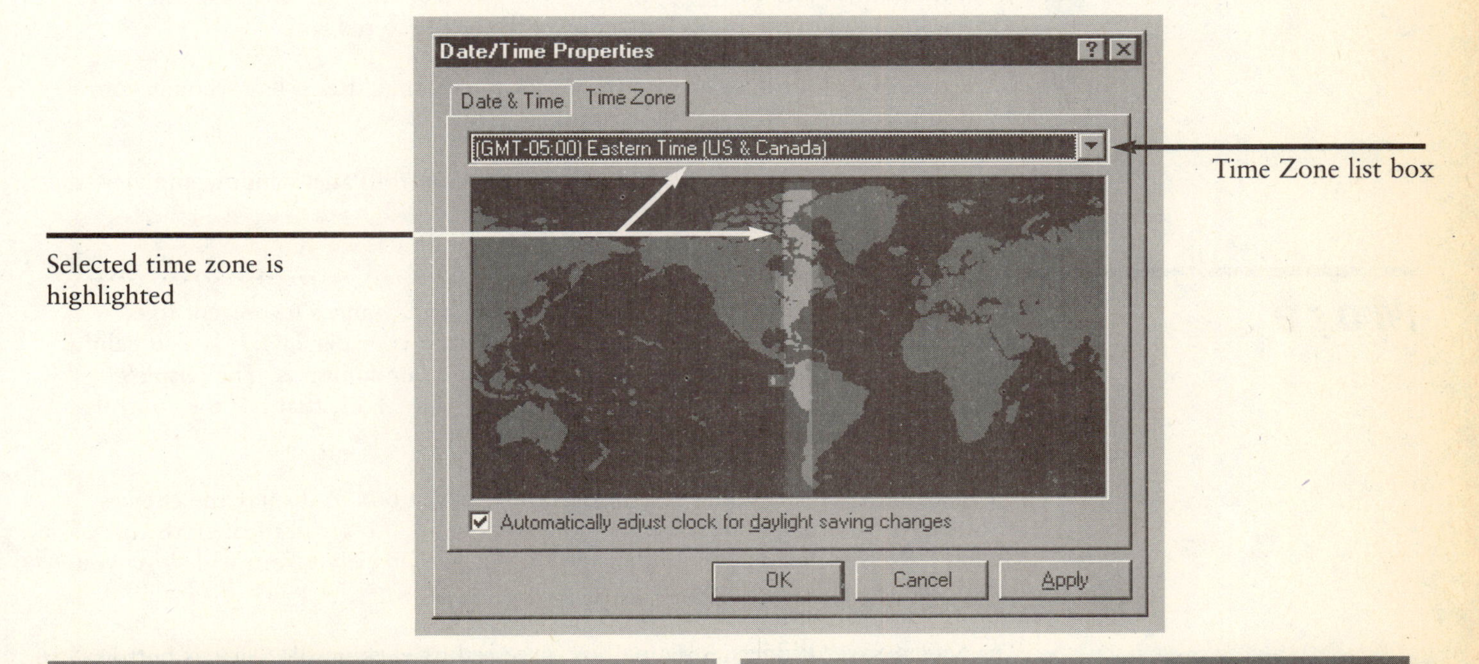

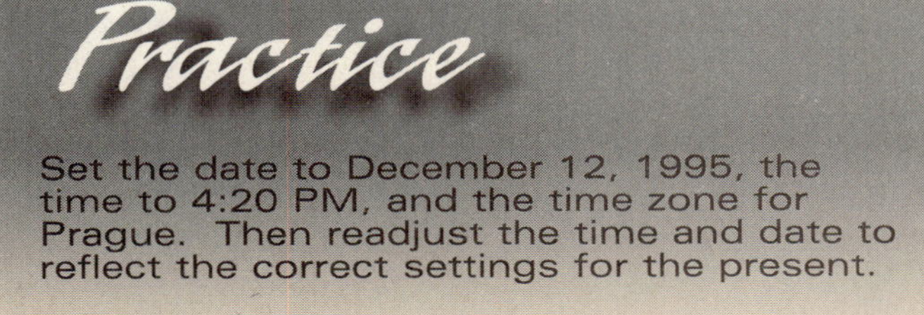

Practice

Set the date to December 12, 1995, the time to 4:20 PM, and the time zone for Prague. Then readjust the time and date to reflect the correct settings for the present.

Hot Tip

Double-clicking the time on the Taskbar will bring up the Date/Time dialog box.

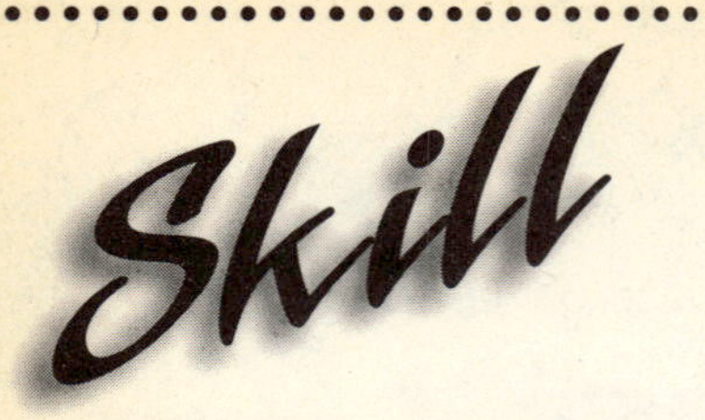

Customizing: The Display

Concept

Windows 95 allows you to change the look of the desktop to suit your personal taste. The Display Properties dialog box has four file tabs that hold the controls for modifying the **Background**, **Screen Saver**, **Appearance** of windows, and monitor **Settings**. The Background tab contains two lists: **Patterns** and **Wallpaper**. A Pattern is a design that can be used to decorate your desktop. You can use a pattern as is or modify it. Wallpaper is a picture that you can use to adorn your desktop.

Do It!

Mike wants to change the Pattern on his desktop to red plaid.

1. Open the **Display Properties** dialog box from the Control Panel. The Background tab will appear at the front of the stack, as shown in Figure 3-9.

2. To change the Pattern you must scroll through the pattern list. Typing the first letter of a word you are searching for in a list box will jump to the words that begin with that letter. Type a [**P**]; Plaid will become highlighted and the preview screen in the dialog box will change to plaid.

3. Click the **Appearance** tab to bring it to the front of the stack.

4. Click the **Color** button, shown in Figure 3-10, and then click the **red** box. The background of the preview window will change to red.

5. Click the **Apply** button to change the desktop pattern. After a few seconds your desktop will change to a red plaid pattern.

6. Click the Minimize button to minimize the Control Panel window and view the desktop pattern change.

More

A **screen saver** is an image or picture that moves and changes to prevent fixed images from becoming permanently embedded onto your display. It is also helpful for covering your work when you are away from your computer. The Display Properties dialog box contains a tab, shown in Figure 3-11, that has the controls for your screen saver.

To change the screen saver, click the **Screen Saver** list box to display the choices installed on your computer. Use the down arrow [↓] to scroll through the list of options. Notice that as you go through the list, the preview screen will show you what each screen saver looks like.

The **Screen Saver Properties** dialog box, accessed by clicking the Settings button, will give you options, such as speed and number of components, for customizing a particular screen saver. To see the screen saver in action, click the Preview button. Be careful not to move the mouse after you do so, as this deactivates the screen saver. Your screen saver will not activate until a certain amount of idle time (time when the mouse is not moved and no keys are pressed) passes. The number in the Wait box determines how much idle time must pass.

You must click **Apply** to turn on a particular screen saver.

Figure 3-9 Display Properties dialog box: Background tab

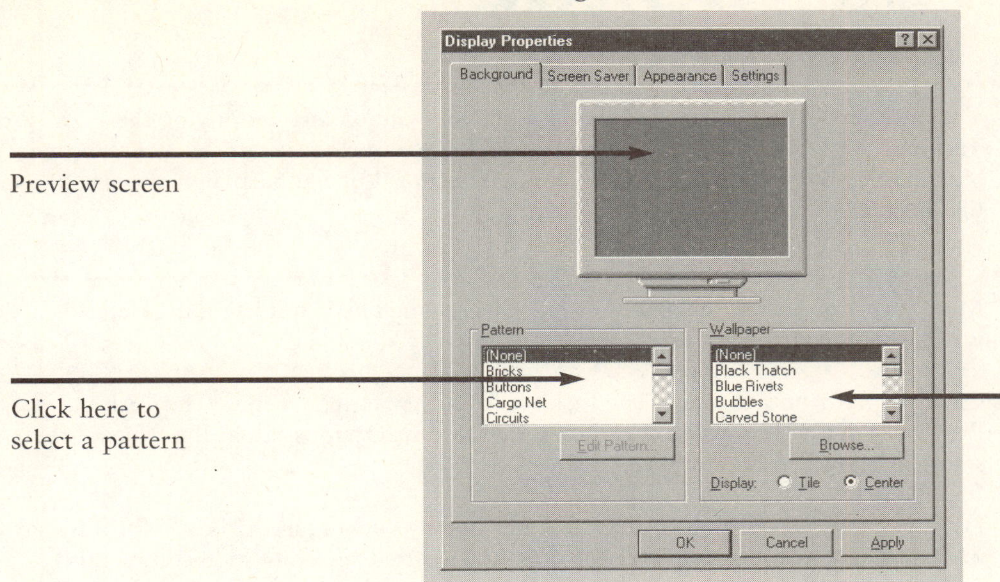

Figure 3-10 Display Properties dialog box: Appearance tab

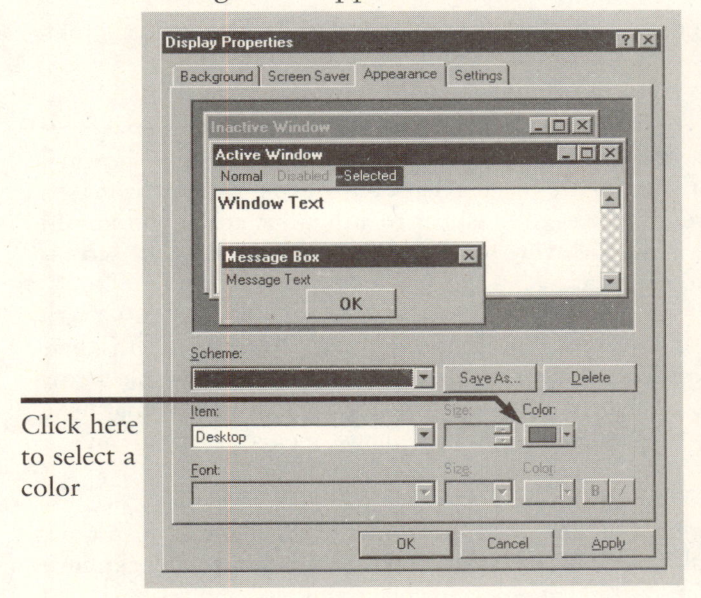

Figure 3-11 Display Properties dialog box: Screen Saver tab

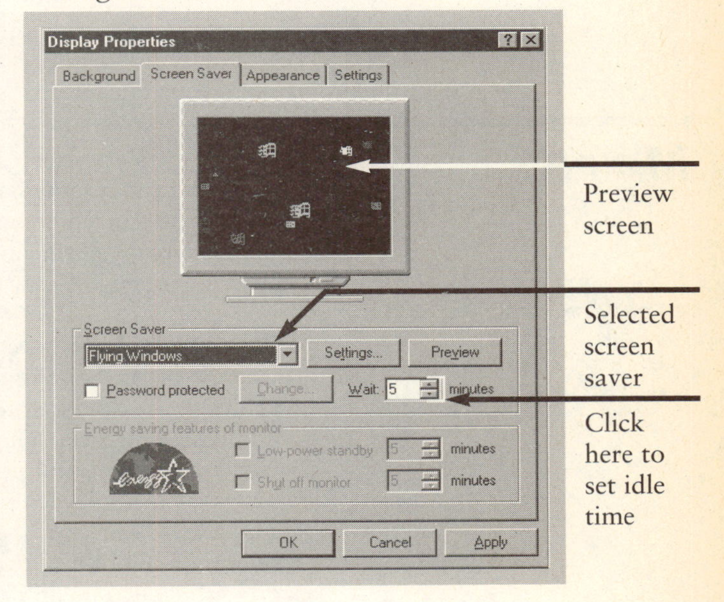

Practice

Set up a screen saver of your choice from the Display Properties dialog box with a one-minute Wait time and preview it. Then reset the Display Properties Background settings to their previous Pattern or Wallpaper.

Hot Tip

To shortcut to the Display Properties dialog box, right-click an empty space on your desktop and select Properties from the pop-up menu.

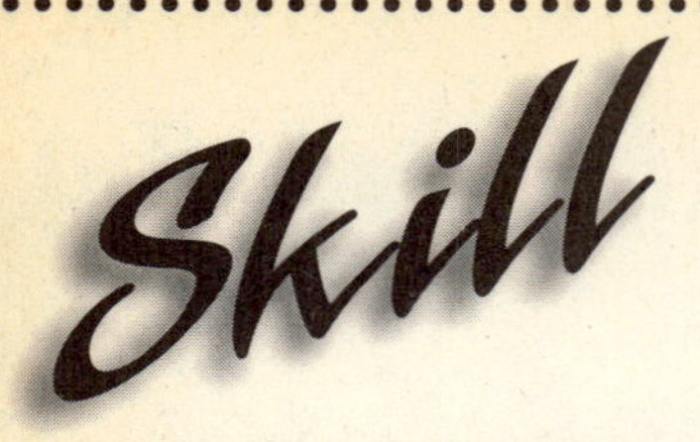

Customizing: The Taskbar

Concept

The Taskbar Properties dialog box contains four options for modifying the **Taskbar**. You can change where and when it appears, the size of the icons on the Start menu, and whether the clock is visible or not. You can also alter the size of the Taskbar.

Do It!

Mike wants to set his Taskbar so it hides itself when he is not using it. He also wants small icons on his Start menu.

1. Click the **Start** button and select Taskbar from the Settings menu. The Taskbar Properties dialog box will appear with the Taskbar Options tab at the front of the stack, as shown in Figure 3-12.

2. Put a mark in the check box next to **Auto hide** by clicking in the box. The Taskbar in the preview window will disappear, indicating that the Auto hide command is on.

3. Click the box next to Show small icons in the Start menu to put a check mark there. The Start menu, icons and all, will be reduced in size.

4. Click the **Apply** button to change the Taskbar settings. The Taskbar will sink out of sight.

More

Most systems are set up so the Taskbar is always on top and the clock is showing. Always on top means that you can see the Taskbar even when a window is maximized. The Auto hide option reduces the Taskbar to a thin line at the bottom of the desktop when it is not is use. Moving the pointer to the bottom of the screen causes a hidden Taskbar to reappear.

Like a window, the Taskbar is not fixed in location or size. To resize the Taskbar, place the pointer on the top edge of the Taskbar. It will change to a double arrow [↕]. With the double-arrow cursor you can drag the top edge of the Taskbar up and increase its size. This is useful when you have many open applications and want to view their full program buttons.

The Taskbar can also be placed on any of the four sides of the desktop. Click and hold the pointer on a blank space on the Taskbar and then drag it to any extremity you wish. Then it can be resized. Figure 3-13 displays a moved and resized Taskbar.

Figure 3-12 Taskbar Properties dialog box

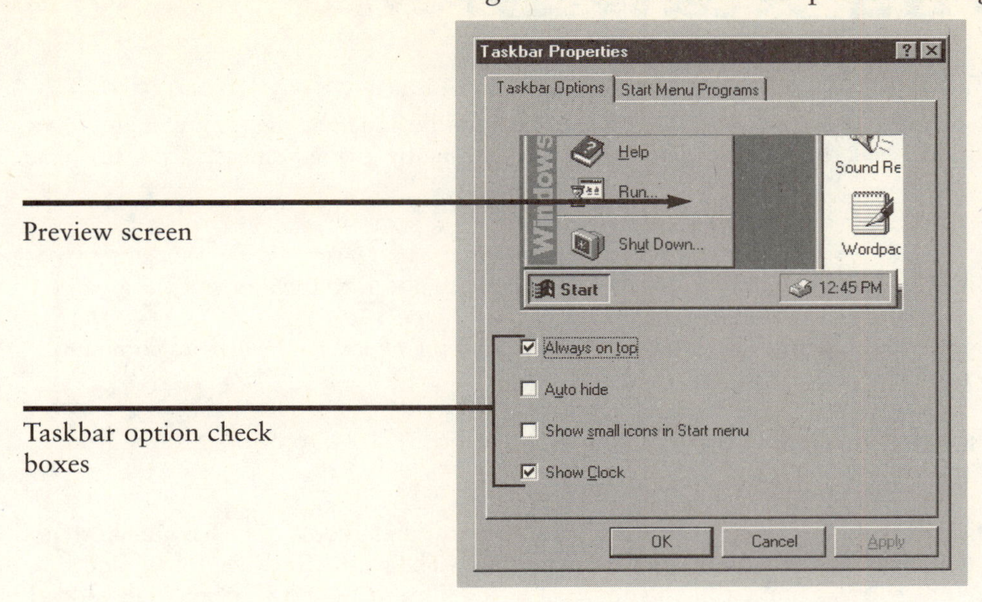

Figure 3-13 Moved and resized Taskbar

Practice

Open WordPad, move the Taskbar to the left side of the desktop, and expand it so you can see the full program button. Return the Taskbar to its previous size and location when you are done.

Hot Tip

If Auto hide is on and you want the Taskbar available even when a window is maximized, make sure the Always on top check box in the Taskbar Properties dialog box is checked.

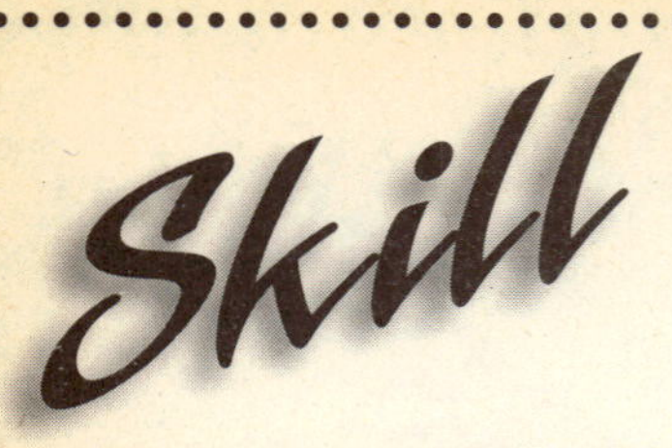

Customizing: The Start Menu

Concept

Frequently used programs, folders, and files can be added to the Start menu. **Adding items to the Start menu** can save you time by giving you easy access to them.

Do It!

Mike uses the Calculator every day and wants to add it to the Start menu.

1. Right-click an empty space on the Taskbar and then click the **Properties** command to open the Taskbar Properties dialog box.

2. Click the **Start Menu Programs** tab, shown in Figure 3-14, to bring it to the front of the stack.

3. Click the **Add** button to open the **Create Shortcut** dialog box. The Create Shortcut dialog box has a section called **Command** line. The path (the drive, folder, and subfolder that contain a file, in addition to the file's name) for the item being added to the Start menu is to be inserted here.

4. Click the **Browse** button to open the Browse window (Figure 3-15) and search for the path of the **Calculator**.

5. Click the **Look in** drop-down list and select **Maindisk** (C:). The contents of your main hard drive will appear in the window.

6. Double-click the **Windows** folder to bring up its contents in the panel.

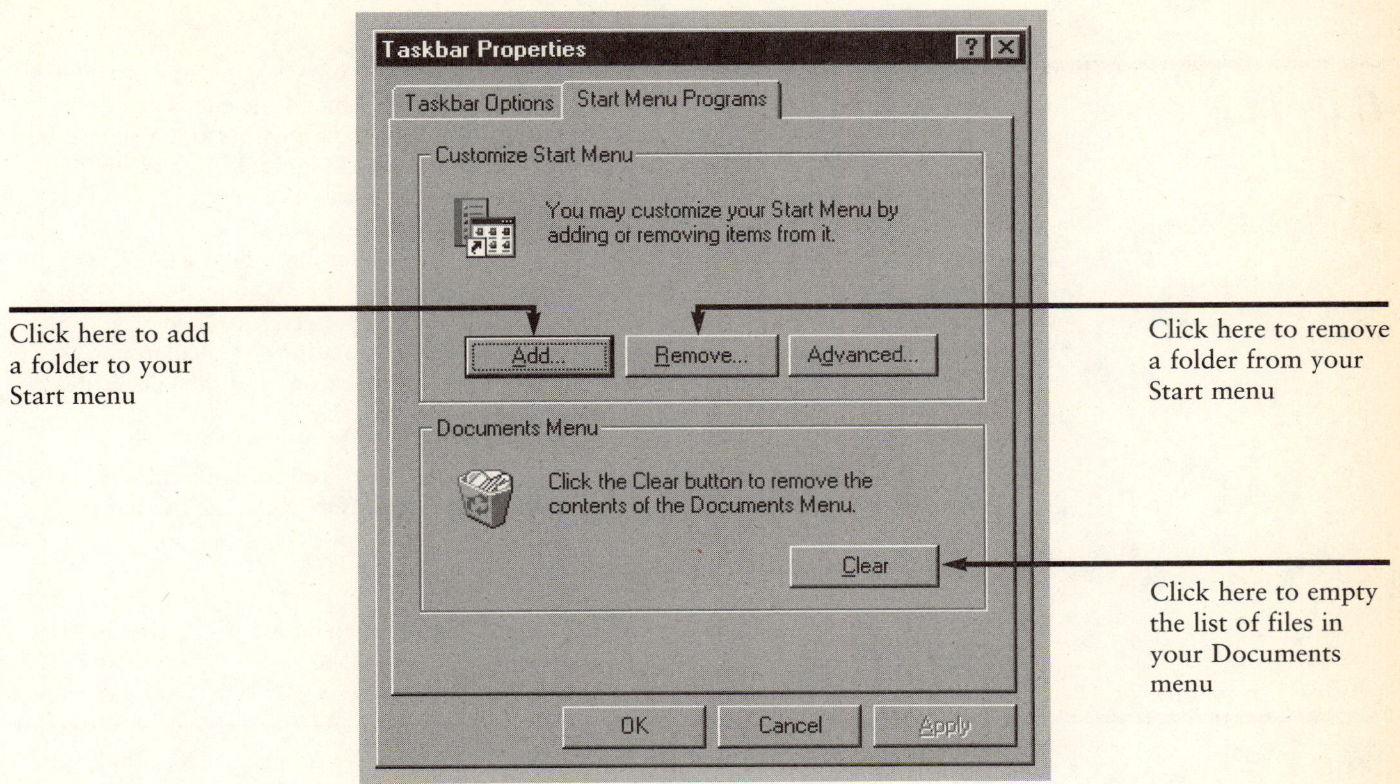

Figure 3-14 Taskbar Properties dialog box: Start Menu Programs tab

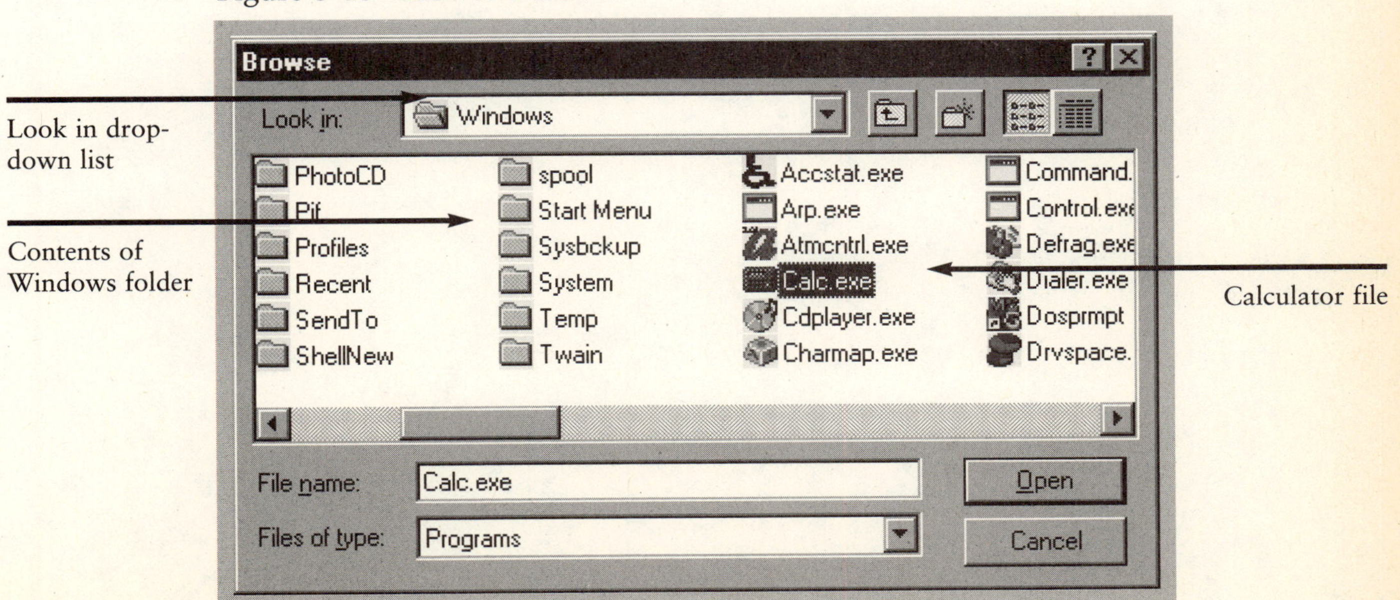

Figure 3-15 Browse window

Customizing: The Start Menu (continued)

Do It!

7. Drag the scroll bar box to the right until the the file named Calc.exe is visible. Click on the **Calc.exe** icon to select it, and then click the **Open** button. You will be returned to the Create Shortcut dialog box, as shown in Figure 3-16, and the path for the Calculator will be in the Command line text box.

8. Click the **Next** button. The **Select Program Folder** dialog box, Figure 3-17, will appear.

9. You can place an item anywhere on the Start menu. To add the Calculator to the first level of the Start menu, click the **Start Menu** folder icon, and then click the **Next** button.

10. The next window, **Select a Title for the Program**, allows you to name the new Start menu item. Calc.exe appears by default. Type **Calculator** to change the name.

11. Click **Finish** to add the Calculator to the Start menu.

12. Click the **Start** button to see that the Calculator has been added to the first level of the Start menu.

More

The Start Menu Programs tab also allows you to remove programs from the Start menu. The **Remove Shortcuts/Folders** window appears when the Remove button is clicked. Simply click the item you wish to take off the Start menu, and then click Remove.

You can empty the Document menu, a list of recently opened files that appears on the Start menu, by clicking the **Clear** button from the Start Menu Programs tab.

Figure 3-16 Create Shortcut dialog box

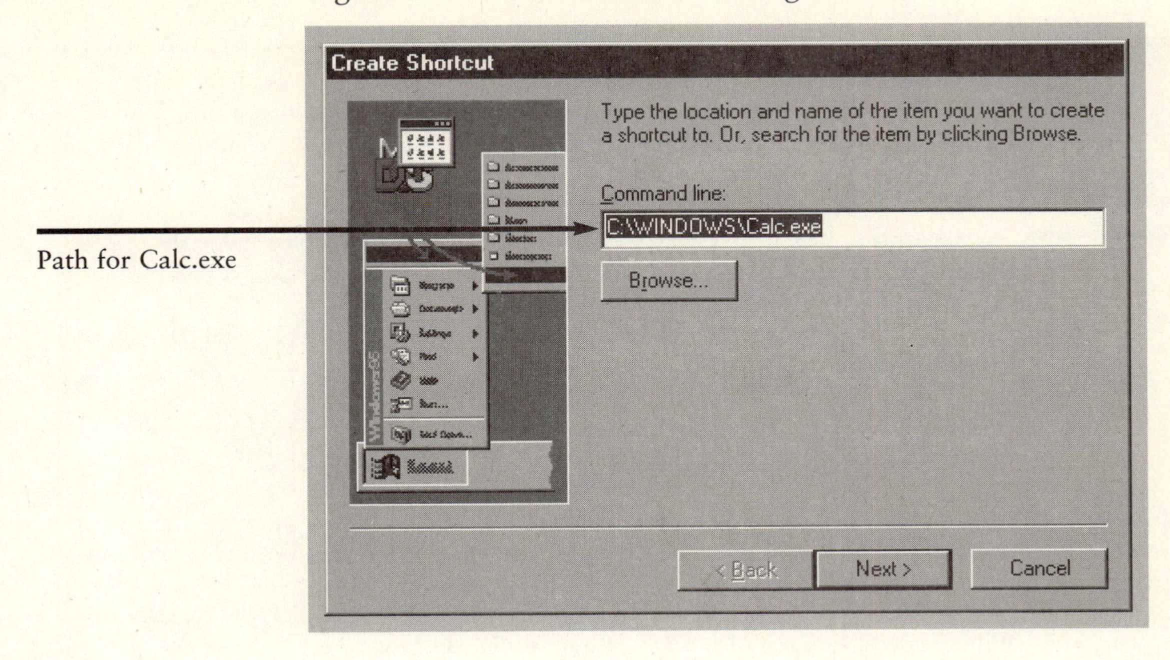

Figure 3-17 Select Program Folder dialog box

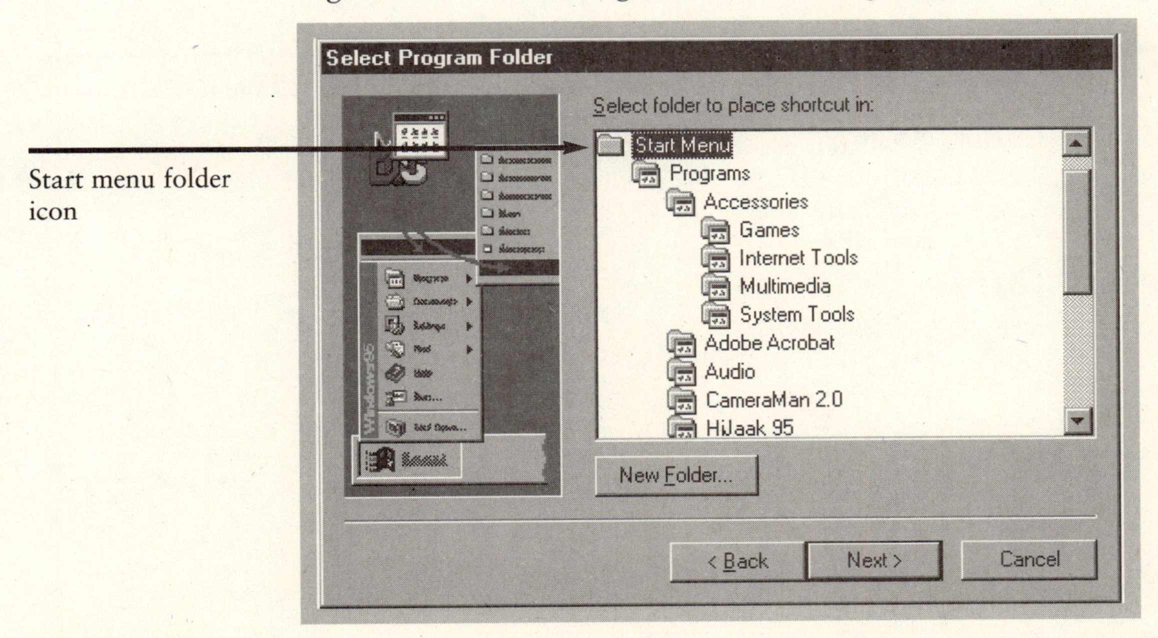

Add WordPad to the first level of the Start menu by going through the Taskbar Properties dialog box. Then remove WordPad and the Calculator from the Start menu.

Hot Tip

You can add an item to the Start menu by dragging it from the Windows Explorer to the Start menu folder or directly to the Start button.

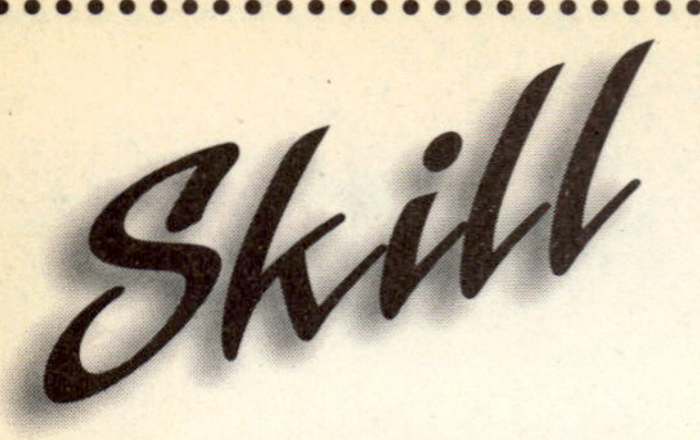

Loading New Software

Concept

Any software package that you buy must be loaded onto your system before you can use it. With a few clicks of the mouse, Windows 95 will load a program for you. The Control Panel contains a tool called **Add/Remove Programs,** which allows for easy installation of new software.

Do It!

Mike wants to walk through the steps of loading new software onto his computer.

1. Click the **Start** button and highlight **Settings**. Select the **Control Panel** to open the Control Panel window.
2. Double-click the **Add/Remove Programs** icon. The Add/Remove Programs Properties dialog box will appear, as shown in Figure 3-18.
3. Click the **Install** button when you are ready to load your new software onto your computer. The **Install Program From Floppy Disk or CD-ROM** window will open.
4. Insert the disk for the new program you want to install and click the **Next** button. Windows will find the disk and run its installation program.
5. Follow any on-screen instructions to complete the installation.

More

You can also install new software by using the **Run** command from the Start menu. Insert the software disk and choose Run from the Start menu. Then type the name of the installation file in the dialog box when prompted, or select Browse and select the installation file from the list given. Windows will open the file you choose and begin loading the application.

Figure 3-18 Add/Remove Programs Properties dialog box

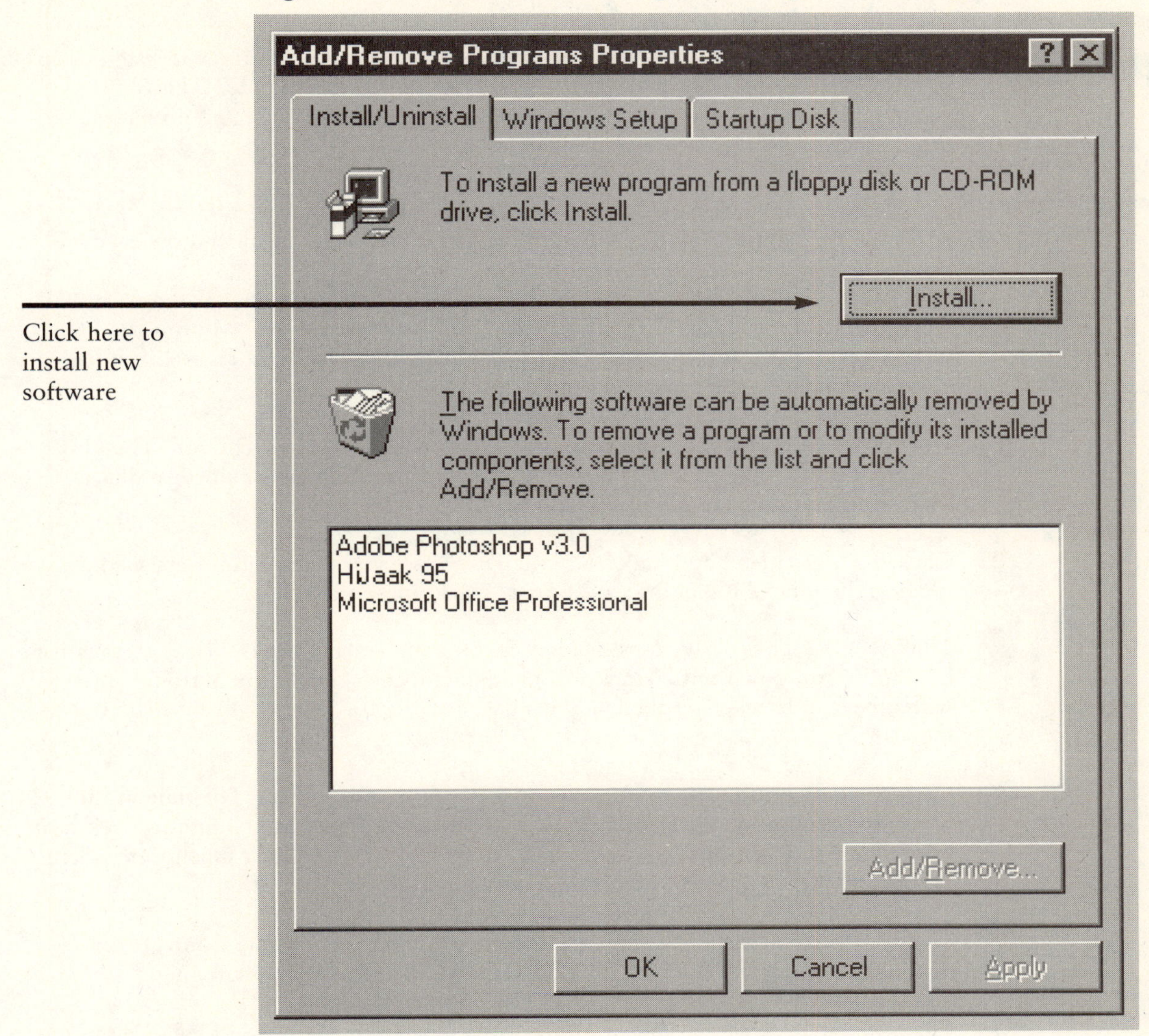

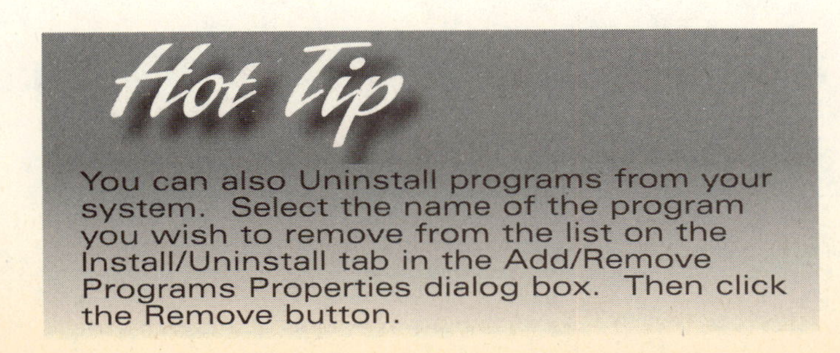

You can also Uninstall programs from your system. Select the name of the program you wish to remove from the list on the Install/Uninstall tab in the Add/Remove Programs Properties dialog box. Then click the Remove button.

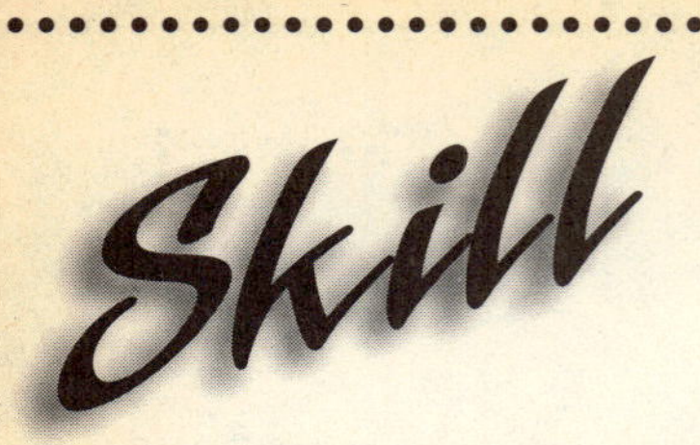

Learning Multimedia

Concept

Windows 95 provides you with four **multimedia** applications. You can listen to an audio CD, record sound, play video clips, and control the volume. This Skill requires that you have a CD drive, an audio card, an audio CD, and an output device such as speakers or headphones.

Do It!

Mike has brought his favorite CD into the office and wants to play it on his computer.

1. Click the **Start** menu, highlight **Programs**, then **Accessories**, then **Multimedia**. Click **CD Player** to open the CD Player window. The window seen in Figure 3-19 has controls similar to the ones found on a real CD player.

2. Open your **CD drive** (D:), insert your CD, and then close the CD door. The play button and the forward and reverse buttons will change from dimmed to black, indicating that you can now use these controls.

3. Click the **View** menu and make sure the Disc/Track info command is checked. If it's not, then move the pointer over **Disc/Track info** and click once.

4. The Track list box allows for quick access to a particular track. Click the **Track** list box and scroll down until **Track 3** is highlighted; click the mouse button. Three [3] will appear in brackets in the black display, and the track time will show between the arrows.

5. Click the **Play** button ▶ to listen to track number three. The time in the black display box will begin counting up, letting you know how long the track has been playing. Click once on this display to get a reading of how much time is left on a track. Click again to display the time remaining on the CD.

6. To adjust the volume, click the **View** menu and select the **Volume Control** command. The Volume Control dialog box, shown in Figure 3-20, will open.

7. The Volume Control dialog box allows you change the volume and balance of any sound device you have installed. Drag the slider for the main volume control, the leftmost panel, up and down until you find an acceptable level. From the control in the CD panel you can further fine-tune the volume.

8. Click the **Stop** button ■, then the **Eject** button ⏏. Remove your CD from the CD drive, close the door, and, finally, close the CD Player window with the **Close** button.

More Features of Windows 95 Multimedia Applications

application	features
CD Player	Plays audio CDs: You can set a play list, play tracks in random order, or preview all tracks on a disc
Media Player	Plays and edits video and audio clips, wave files, and MIDI files
Sound Recorder	Records and stores sound files: you can record straight from an audio CD, save the file, and even paste it into another document
Volume Control	Changes the sound and balance levels for all of the audio devices on your computer

Figure 3-19 CD Player controls

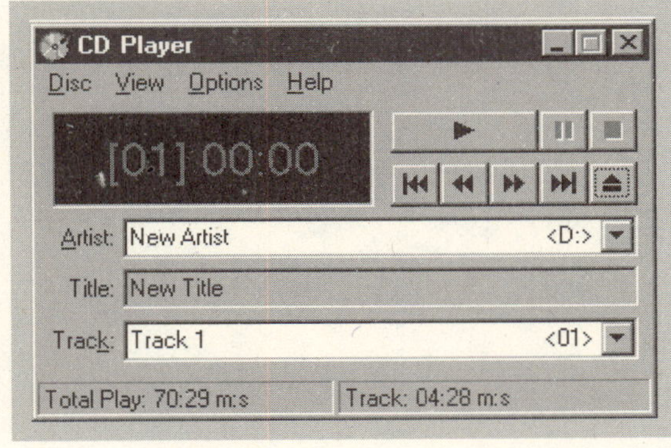

Figure 3-20 Volume Control dialog box

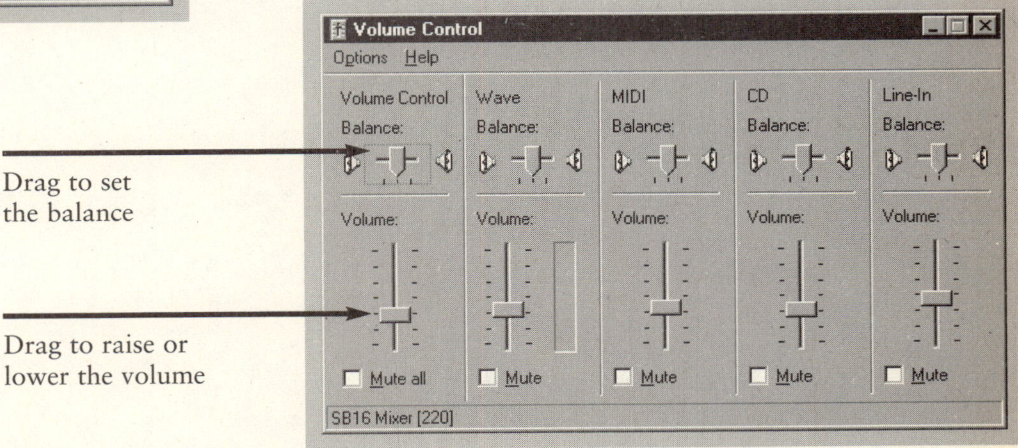

Practice

Set up the play list for your CD: Click the Disc menu and then select the Edit Play List command. Enter the artist, title, and track names where prompted. Click the OK button to save your set list. Eject, then reinsert your CD to see that the list is saved.

Hot Tip

Double-clicking on the speaker icon next to the clock on the Taskbar will open the Volume Control dialog box. A single click will open just the main volume panel.

Shortcuts

Function	Button/Mouse	Menu	Keyboard
Open the Control Panel	Click the Start button, highlight Settings, click Control Panel		[Alt] + [S], [S], [C]
Change the back-ground and screen saver	Click Start, highlight Settings, click Control Panel, double-click the Display icon		
Customize the Taskbar	Move the pointer on the Taskbar and drag the border to enlarge or shrink, or drag the Taskbar to move it	Right-click the Taskbar, click Properties	[Alt] + [S], [S], [T]
Add an item to the Start menu	Drag item to the Start button	Click Start, highlight Settings, click Taskbar, then click the Start menu programs tab	
Add new software	Click the Start button, highlight Settings, click the Control Panel, then double-click the Add/Remove Programs icon		[Alt] + [S], [S], [C], arrow to Add/Remove Programs icon, [Enter]

Identify Key Features

Figure 3-21

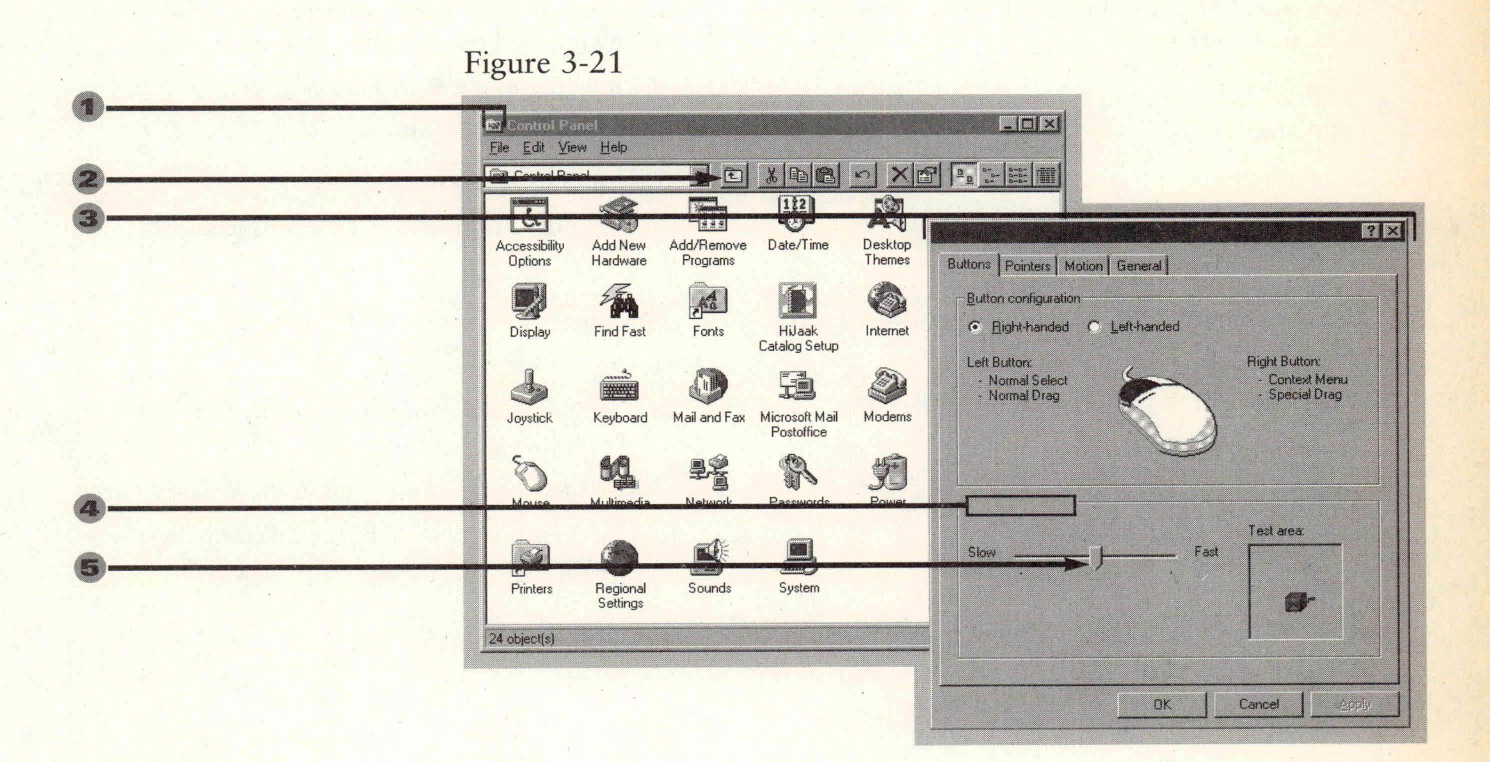

Select the Best Answer

6. Keeps images from getting burned into your display
7. Where you select a time zone
8. Contains icons that allow you to customize your Windows setup
9. Where you can add frequently used files or folders
10. Option that makes it easier to see your pointer as it moves across the screen

a. Date/Time Properties
b. Control Panel
c. Screen saver
d. Pointer trails
e. Start menu

Quiz (continued)

Complete the Statement

11. The control for the double-click speed of your mouse is located on the:
    a. Buttons tab
    b. Pointers tab
    c. Motion tab
    d. General tab

12. You can change all of the following Taskbar properties except:
    a. Size
    b. Location on the desktop
    c. Color
    d. Whether it is hidden or not

13. The Printers window can be used to:
    a. Print a document
    b. Select a printer
    c. Pause your computer
    d. Create a document

14. Items can be added to the Start menu by all of the following methods except:
    a. Dragging to the Start button
    b. Using the Taskbar Properties dialog box
    c. Using the Windows Explorer
    d. Using the Add/Remove Programs icon

15. To change the color of your desktop:
    a. Use the Paint program
    b. Change the desktop pattern in the Display Properties dialog box
    c. Use the Change Color icon in the Control Panel
    d. Use the Appearance tab in the Display Properties dialog box

Interactivity

Test Your Skills

1. Change the color and pattern on your desktop:
   a. Right-click a blank space on the desktop and select Properties from the pop-up menu.
   b. From the Background tab select a pattern that you like.
   c. Click the Appearance tab.
   d. Click the Color button and select a new color.
   e. Click the Apply button to change the look of your desktop.

2. Change the Taskbar settings and then move and resize it:
   a. Click the Start button, highlight Settings, and select Taskbar.
   b. Put a check next to all the Taskbar options.
   c. Open WordPad by clicking the Start button, highlighting Programs and then Accessories, and selecting WordPad.
   d. Drag the Taskbar to the left side of your screen.
   e. Resize the Taskbar so you can see all of the WordPad program button.
   f. Maximize WordPad.
   g. Activate the Taskbar and then drag it back to the bottom of your screen.
   h. Close WordPad.

3. Add WordPad to the first level of the Start menu:
   a. Right-click the Taskbar and select Properties from the pop-up menu.
   b. Click the Start Menu Programs tab.
   c. Click the Add button.
   d. Click the Browse button in the Create Shortcut dialog box.
   e. In the Browse dialog box select the C: disk from the Look in drop-down list, and then double-click the Program Files icon.
   f. Double-click the Accessories folder, then WordPad.
   g. Click the Next button.
   h. Select the Start menu folder, then click the Next button.
   i. Click the Finish button to add WordPad to the Start Menu.

Interactivity (continued)

Test Your Skills

4. Remove WordPad from the Start Menu:
    a. Right-click the Taskbar and select Properties from the pop-up menu.
    b. Click the Start Menu Programs tab.
    c. Click the Remove button.
    d. Click the WordPad icon, and then click the Remove button.
    e. Close all open windows.

Problem Solving

It is March 7, 1999, and large chunks of asteroid have been unearthed in Kabul. The science department of the university you work for has sent you there to help with their expedition to examine the pieces. It is your job to customize all of the computers they are using. Due to budget cutbacks they are still running Windows 95. It is 11:45 AM.

Now begin to make the following changes to the default settings:

1. Open the Control Panel.
2. Double-click the Date/Time icon and set the date, time, and time zone so it is correct.
3. Double-click the Display icon and set the desktop pattern and the background color to a selection of your choosing.
4. Pick a screen saver and set it go on after two minutes of idle time.
5. Close the Control Panel.
6. Right-click the Taskbar and select Properties.
7. Set the Taskbar so it is always on top, auto hides, and shows the clock.
8. Move the Taskbar to the top of the screen.

- ▶ Opening and Renaming a WordPad Document
- ▶ Editing in WordPad
- ▶ Formatting a Document in WordPad
- ▶ Printing a WordPad Document
- ▶ Using Paint
- ▶ Advanced Paint Functions
- ▶ Sharing Data Between Applications

LESSON 4

WINDOWS PROGRAMS

Windows 95 comes with a simple word processing program called WordPad and a drawing program called Paint. These applications are useful for helping you complete many of your day-to-day tasks.

Word processors such as WordPad are great tools for creating documents. They allow you to store multiple copies of a file in progress so you can make changes to one version without disrupting your original. Editing is simple using cut, copy, and paste techniques, and formatting can be added to make a document more visually appealing.

Paint is a program that is useful for working with images. You can create simple or complex pictures with this application. Paint contains a large color palette and many drawing tools. It also includes a full range of manipulation commands useful for stretching, skewing, and rotating images.

An advanced feature of Windows 95 is the ability to easily share data between programs. At the end of this lesson you will help Mike insert his company logo into a WordPad document.

Opening and Renaming a WordPad Document

Concept

You have used WordPad in Lesson 1 to insert Mike's name and the date into a blank document. This lesson will teach you about some of the **more advanced functions of WordPad**. Just as you must open a program in order to use it, you must also open a file to create a new document. Renaming a file allows you to make changes while keeping the original intact.

Do It!

Mike wants to open a letter he has written to his clients and will save it under a new name.

1. Click the **Start** button, highlight **Programs,** then **Accessories**, and click **WordPad.** WordPad will open with a blank document window.
2. Click the **Open** button on the toolbar. The Open dialog box will appear, as shown in Figure 4-1. It is helpful to know your file hierarchy so you can easily locate the folder in which the document is stored.
3. Click the **Look in** drop-down list and select the drive that your student files are located in: Select 3½ Floppy (A:) if your student files are on a floppy disk or Maindisk (C:) if they are stored on your hard drive. All of the folders for the drive you choose will be listed in the window.
4. Click your **Student Folder**, then click the **Open** button. The contents of your Student Folder will appear in the window.
5. Double-click the file named **L4-A**. The file will open and appear as a document in the WordPad window.
6. Click the **File** menu and then select the **Save As** command. The Save As dialog box (Figure 4-2) will open.
7. When the dialog box opens, the file name **L4-A** will be highlighted in the **File name** text box, ready to accept a new name. Type **Client Letter** and click the **Save** button to store the document under a different name. The title bar will now read Client Letter, reflecting the change of name.
8. Do not close WordPad or the Client Letter; you will use them in the next Skill.

More

WordPad Toolbar Buttons

button		function
New		Creates a new, blank WordPad document
Open		Opens a saved WordPad document
Save		Stores the active WordPad document with its current file name
Print		Prints one copy of the active WordPad document using the current printer settings
Preview		Shows how the active document will look when printed
Find		Searches for specified text in a document
Cut		Removes selected text and sends it to the Clipboard
Copy		Copies selected text and sends it to the Clipboard
Paste		Inserts the contents of the Clipboard at the insertion point
Undo		Reverses the last action performed
Date/Time		Opens the Date/Time dialog box

Figure 4-1 Open dialog box

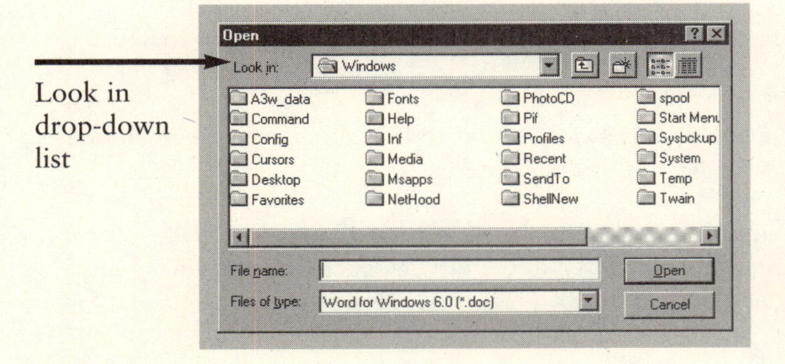

Figure 4-2 Save As dialog box

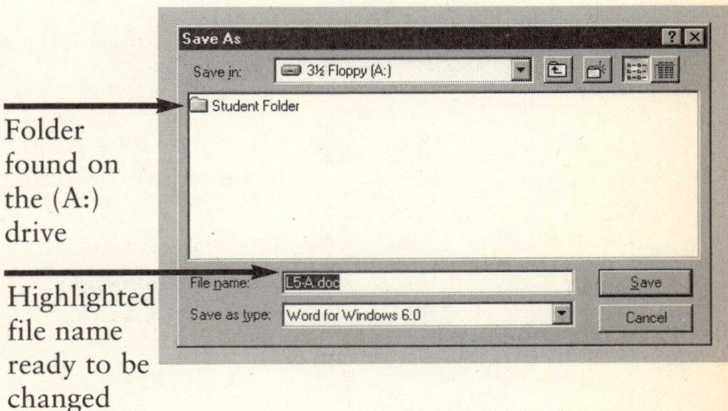

Practice

Open the file named Shopping List from the To Do folder in your student files and rename it Grocery.

Hot Tip

A renamed file does not have to be stored in the same place as the original. From the Save in drop-down list you can select any drive or folder in which you wish to store a document.

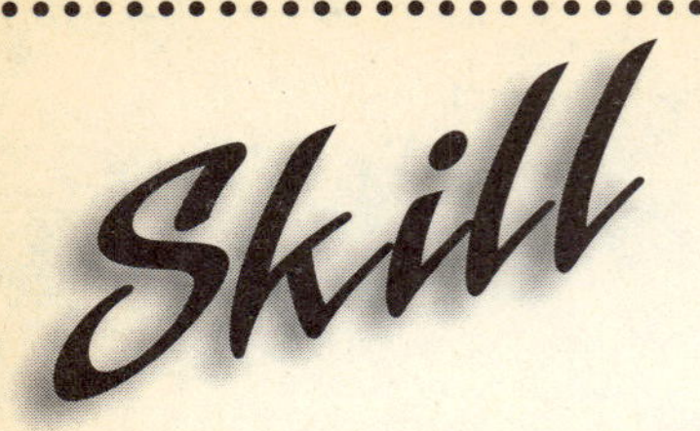

Editing in WordPad

Concept

WordPad allows you to **edit** text without having to retype the entire document. WordPad's editing features enable you to easily change the spelling of a word and to move sections of text using cut and paste procedures.

Do It!

Mike needs to edit a letter he has written to his clients. He wants to correct spelling errors, change a word, and move a sentence.

1. In the second sentence of the first paragraph the word "larger" has been spelled incorrectly. Use the mouse to move the I-beam between the two g's of the word "lagger" and then click once. A flashing cursor will appear between the "g's" indicating the insertion point.

2. Press [**Backspace**] to delete the character to the left of the insertion point.

3. Type an [**r**]. "Lager" will now read "larger."

4. In the third sentence of the first paragraph replace "vehicle" with "truck" by first moving the I-beam to the left of "vehicle." Click once to move the insertion point.

5. Drag the cursor over the entire word "vehicle" to highlight it. Highlighted, or selected, text is ready to be edited. In this case it will be written over when you begin to type.

6. Type **truck** to change the text.

7. Move the I-beam to the left of the word "Thank" in the first sentence of the letter and click once to move the insertion point.

8. Drag the cursor over the entire sentence to highlight it and prepare the sentence to be moved.

9. Click the **Cut** button to send the selected text to the **Clipboard**. The Clipboard is a temporary storage place for cut or copied items.

10. Text pasted from the Clipboard is placed at the insertion point. Move the insertion point to the right of the word "business" in the last sentence of the letter by moving the mouse pointer there and clicking.

11. Click the **Paste** button to move the text Your letter will look like Figure 4-3.

12. Click the **Save** button to save the changes you have made, then leave the file open for use in the next Skill.

More

Keyboard Keys Used to Move Around a Document

key(s)	moves	key(s)	moves
↑	Up one line	[Home]	To the beginning of the line
↓	Down one line	[End]	To the end of the text line
→	Right one character	[Ctrl] + [Home]	To the beginning of the document
←	Left one character	[Ctrl] + [End]	To the end of the document
[Page Up]	Up to the previous page	[Ctrl] + [→]	One word to the right
[Page Down]	Down to the next page	[Ctrl] + [←]	One word to the left

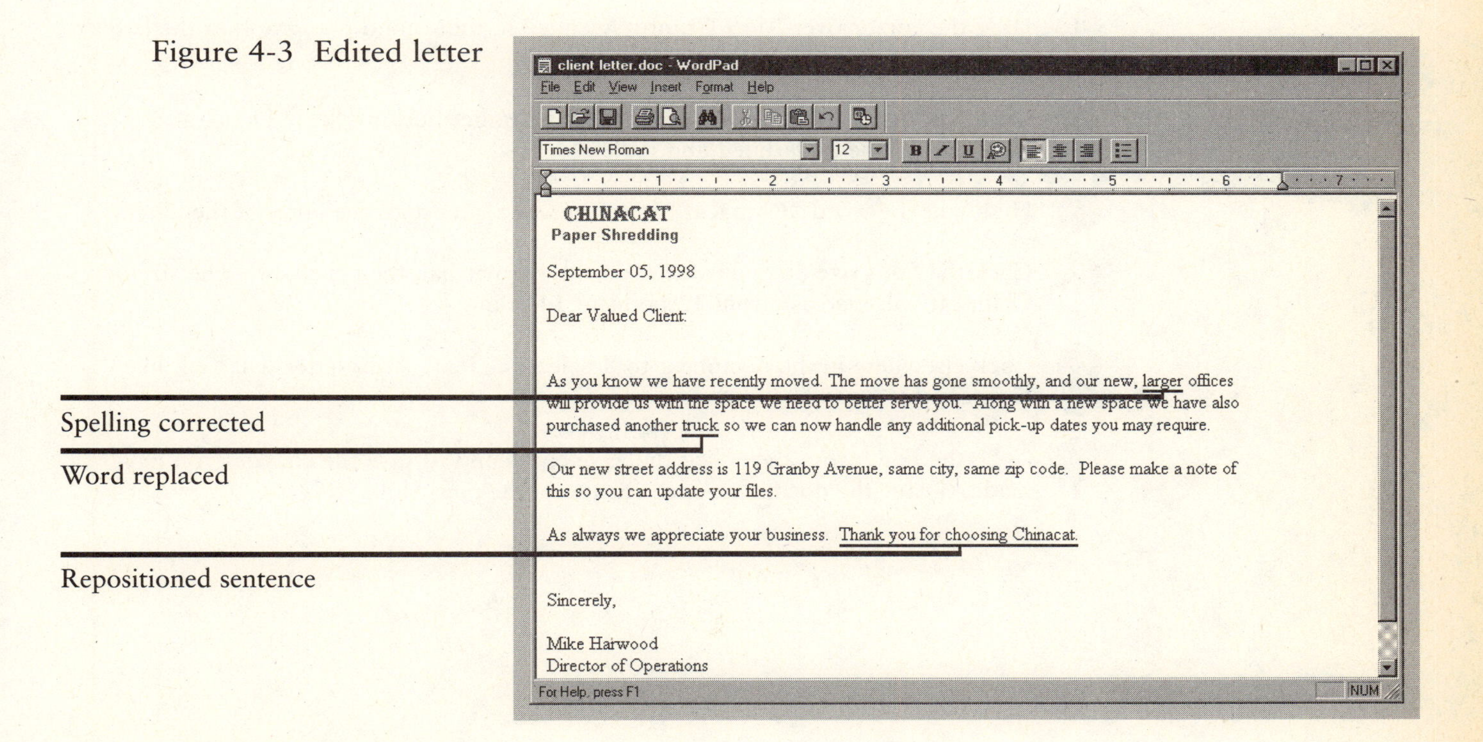

CHINACAT
Paper Shredding

September 05, 1998

Dear Valued Client:

As you know we have recently moved. The move has gone smoothly, and our new, larger offices will provide us with the space we need to better serve you. Along with a new space we have also purchased another truck so we can now handle any additional pick-up dates you may require.

Our new street address is 119 Granby Avenue, same city, same zip code. Please make a note of this so you can update your files.

As always we appreciate your business. Thank you for choosing Chinacat.

Sincerely,

Mike Harwood
Director of Operations

Figure 4-3 Edited letter

Practice

In the Client Letter, cut the paragraph that begins, "As you know we have recently moved," and paste it between the closing and Mike Harwood. Do not save this change.

Hot Tip

Selected text can be moved by dragging it to its desired location.

Formatting a Document in WordPad

Concept

Formatting text changes the way it appears on the page. Formatting can make a document appear more attractive and easier to read.

Do It!

Mike wants to format his Client Letter. He will center his letterhead, underline and italicize his new address, and change the size of the company name font.

1. Make sure the **Format Bar** is displayed. Click **View** and select **Format Bar** if it is not already checked.
2. Drag the I-beam over the Chinacat Paper Shredding letterhead in the upper left corner of the page to highlight it.
3. Click the **Center** button. The highlighted text will move to the middle of the page and the button will remain indented, indicating that particular section of text is formatted for centering.
4. Drag the cursor over "119 Granby Avenue" in the second paragraph of the letter to select it.
5. Click the **Underline** button and then the **Italics** button. "119 Granby Avenue" will be underlined and italicized.
6. Highlight the word "Chinacat" from the last sentence of the body of the letter.
7. Click the **Font size** drop-down list on the Format bar, then click **14**. The size of **Chinacat** will increase from 12 point to 14 point.
8. Click elsewhere in the document to deselect the text. Your letter will look like Figure 4-4.
9. Click the **File** menu, then click the **Save** command to save the changes you have made. Leave the document open for use in the next Skill.

More

Format Bar Button Functions

button	function	button	function
Times New Roman	Changes the font of the selected text		Changes the color of the selected text
12	Changes the size of the font of the selected text		Aligns selected text to the left indent
B	Bolds the selected text		Centers the selected text
/	Italicizes the selected text		Aligns selected text to the right indent or margin
U	Underlines the selected text		Adds bullets to a selected list

Figure 4-4 Formatted letter

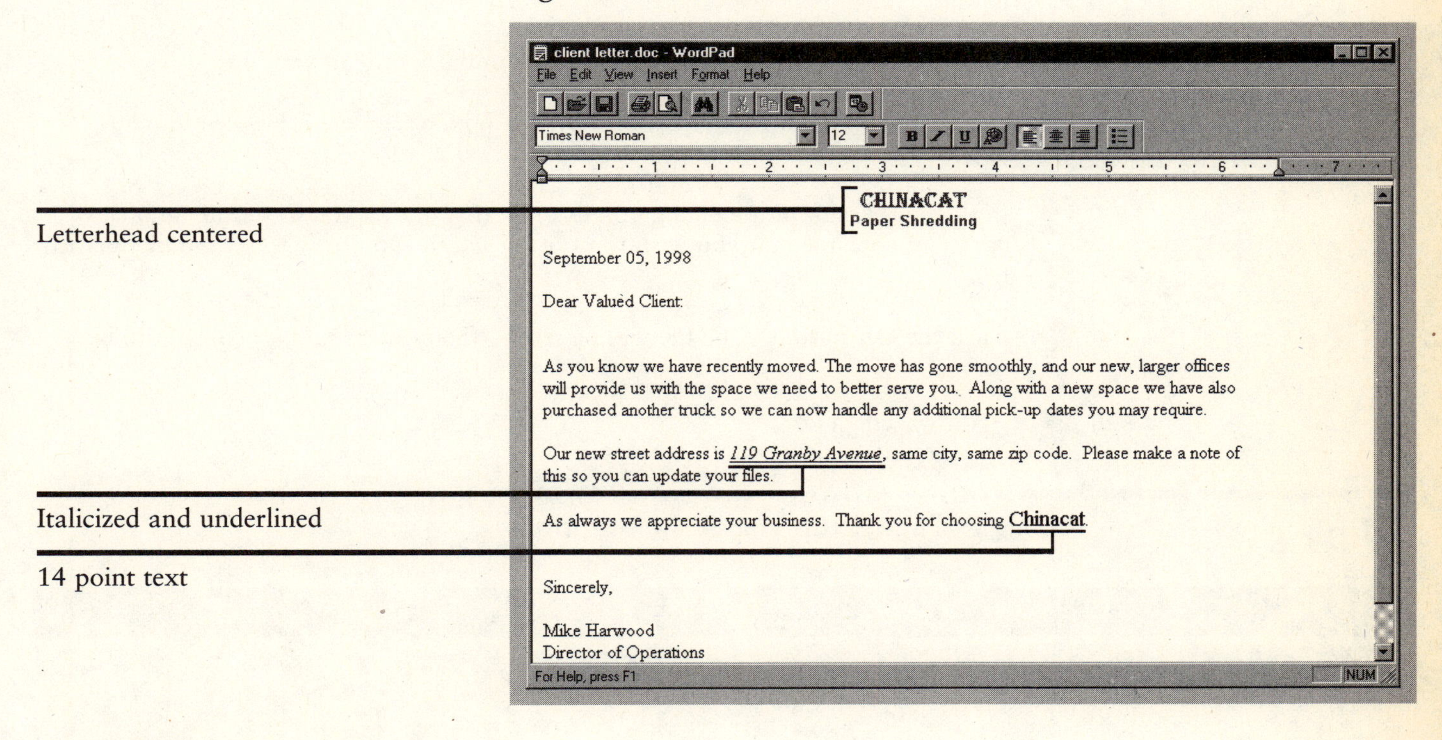

CHINACAT
Paper Shredding

September 05, 1998

Dear Valued Client:

As you know we have recently moved. The move has gone smoothly, and our new, larger offices will provide us with the space we need to better serve you. Along with a new space we have also purchased another truck so we can now handle any additional pick-up dates you may require.

Our new street address is *119 Granby Avenue*, same city, same zip code. Please make a note of this so you can update your files.

As always we appreciate your business. Thank you for choosing Chinacat.

Sincerely,

Mike Harwood
Director of Operations

Practice

Change the entire body of the text to 16 point in the font of your choice and then bold and underline the date. Undo these changes when you are through.

Hot Tip

You can quickly highlight an entire paragraph by triple-clicking.

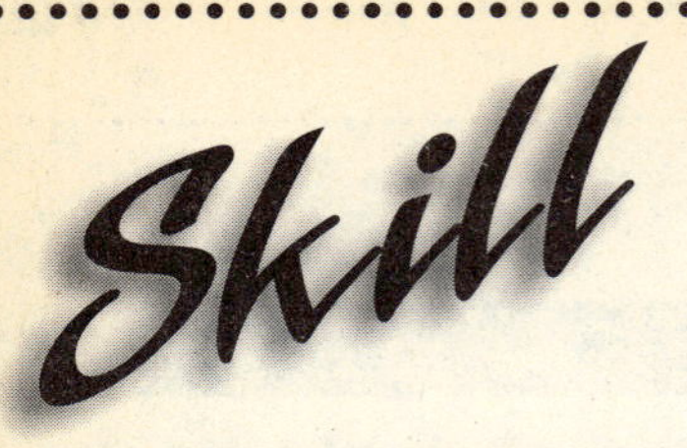

Printing a WordPad Document

Concept

Printing a document transfers what is on your screen to paper. Printing a document is useful when you want to have a hard copy of your information to edit, to pass along to others, or to file away.

Do It!

Mike wants to print two copies of his Client Letter.

1. Click the **File** menu, then select **Print Preview**. The Print Preview window will open, as shown in Figure 4-5. A miniature version of your document will appear, and the mouse pointer will change to the **magnifier** .
2. With the magnifier on the preview page, click the mouse button to **Zoom In**. The small image of the file, shown exactly as it will appear on the printed page, blows up to give you a better view. The horizontal and vertical dashed lines represent the margins.
3. Click the **Close** button [Close] to return to the WordPad window.
4. Click **File** and select **Print**. The Print dialog box, as shown in Figure 4-6, will appear.
5. In the lower right of the dialog box is a box that allows you to set the number of copies of your file that you wish to print. Click the **up** arrow to set the number to [2].
6. Click the **OK** button. The file will be sent to the printer and two copies will be printed.
7. Close WordPad.

More

Page Setup Dialog Box Options

option	Changes
Paper	
Size	The dimensions of the page or envelope you wish to print on
Source	The location of the paper in the printer you are using; some printers have more than one tray
Orientation	The placement of the document on the page
Portrait	Height of the page is greater than width
Landscape	Width of the page is greater than height
Margins	The amount of space between the text and the edge of the page

Figure 4-5 Print Preview window

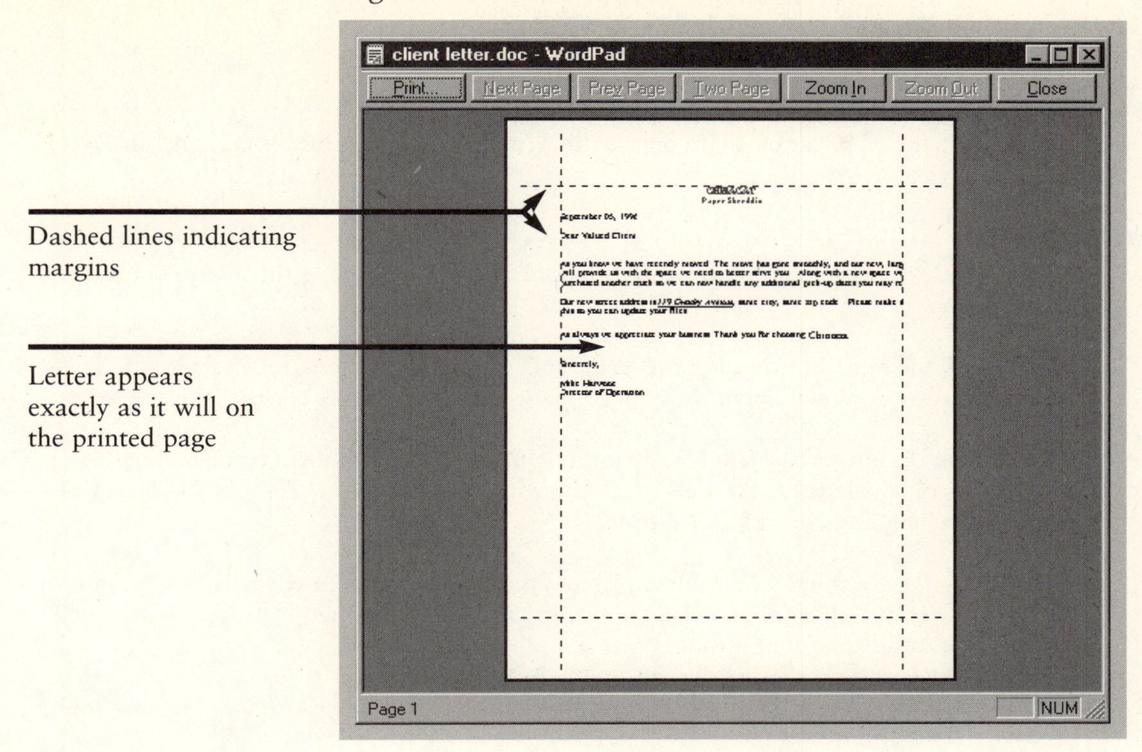

Figure 4-6 Print dialog box

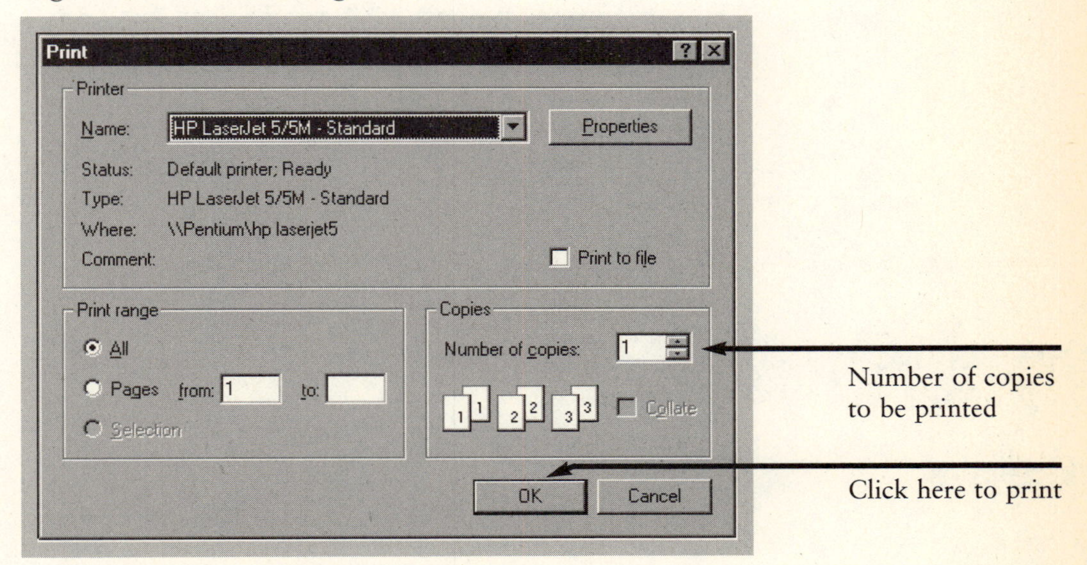

Practice

Change the document to Landscape orientation and print one copy.

Hot Tip

Click the Print button to print one copy of your file with the current print settings, without opening the dialog box.

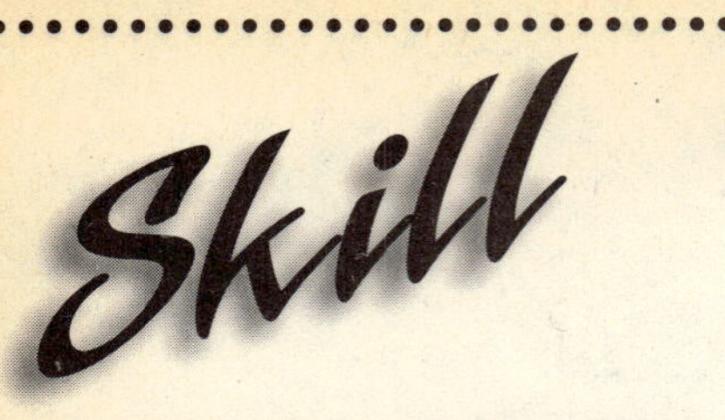

Using Paint

Concept

The **paint** application that comes with Windows 95 is useful for creating and working with images.

Do It!

Mike explores Paint by drawing a square and a circle, filling them with color, and saving the file he creates.

1. Click the **Start** button, point to **Programs**, then **Accessories**, and click **Paint**. The Paint window will open. Maximize the window by double-clicking the title bar.

2. If you do not see the **Tool Box** on the left side of the window, or the **Color Box** (the color palette) at the bottom of the window, then select the Tool Box and Color Box commands from the **View** menu.

3. Click the **Rectangle** tool button and then move the pointer to the lower right of the window. The pointer will change to **crosshairs** when it is over the work space, indicating that a tool is active.

4. Shapes are drawn by dragging the crosshairs across the work space. Clicking the mouse button fixes the starting point of the shape you are drawing. You can change the size of a shape as long as the mouse button is held down. Once you let go of the button, the shape's size will be fixed. Drag the indicator diagonally to the left to draw a square about 2 inches by 2 inches.

5. Click the **Ellipse** tool . This tool allows you to draw circular-shaped objects.

6. Move the crosshairs to the upper left corner of the work space and drag to draw a large circle similar to the one shown in Figure 4-7.

Figure 4-7 Paint window

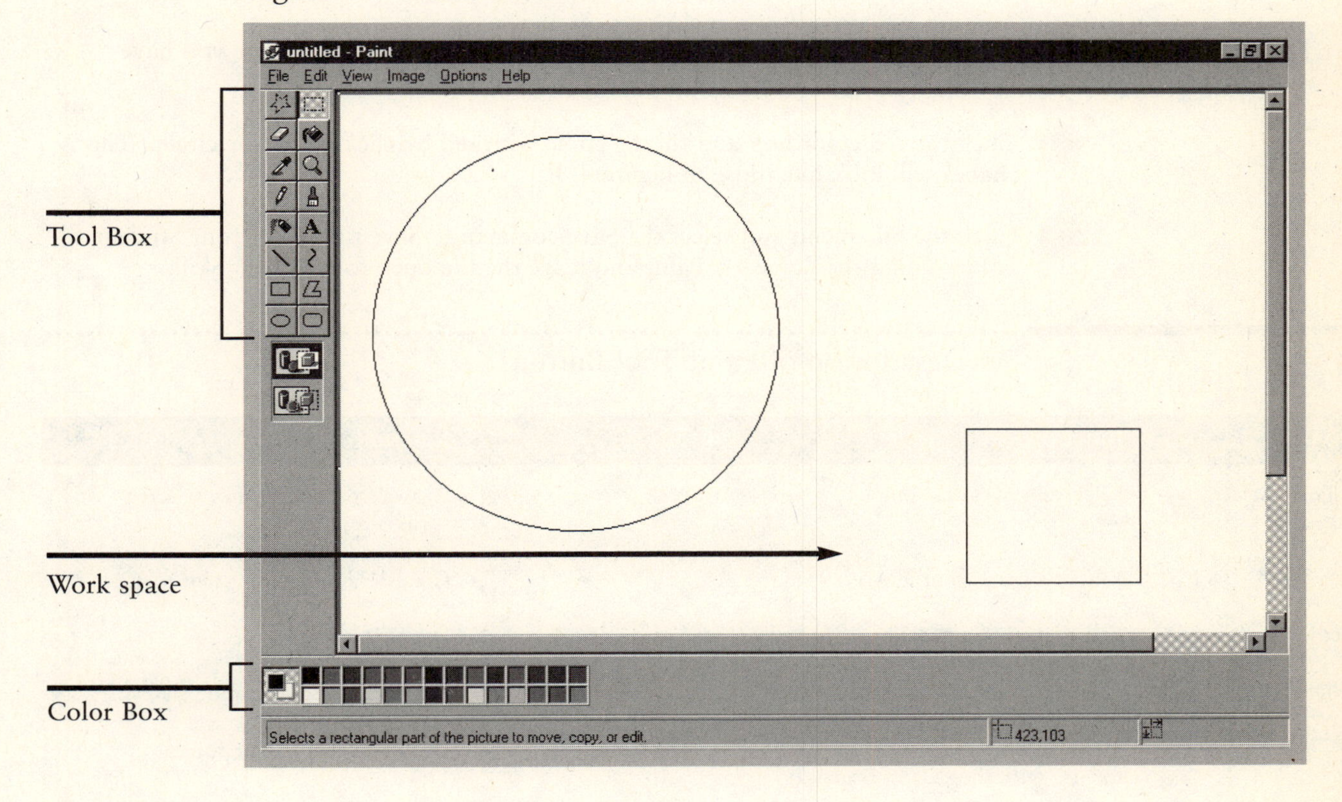

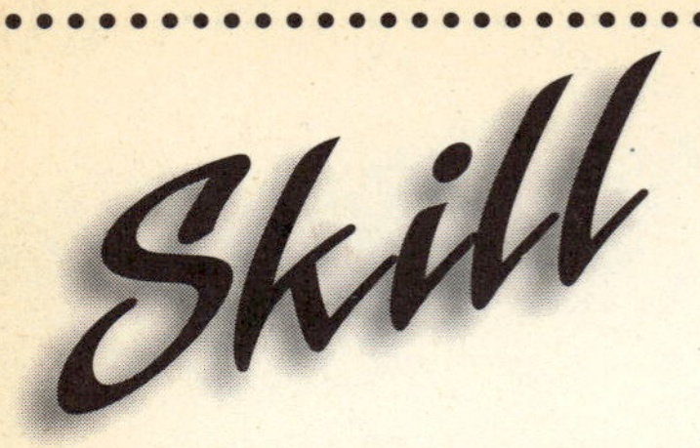

Using Paint (continued)

Do It!

7. Click the **Fill with Color** tool button. The pointer will change to a small jar spilling paint. This tool will fill any area defined by a border with a specified color.

8. Click the **blue color box** and then move the pointer onto the square you have drawn. Click anywhere in the square to fill it with blue.

9. Click the red color box and fill the circle with red by clicking on the circle. The shapes will look like those in Figure 4-8.

10. Click the **File** menu and select the **Save** command. Save the file in your Student Folder under the name 1st Paint and leave the file open for the next Skill.

More

Description of Paint Tool Buttons

button	function	button	function
Free-Form Select	Selects an irregular shape	Airbrush	Draws freehand with a selected spray size
Select	Selects an area on the work space	Text	Creates an insertion point for text
Eraser	Erases part of a drawing	Line	Draws a straight line
Fill With Color	Fills an area with a selected color	Curve	Draws a line that can be shaped
Pick Color	Picks up a color from the picture for use with the Pencil, Brush, or Airbrush tools	Rectangle	Draws a rectangle or square
Magnifier	Zooms in on a part of the drawing	Polygon	Draws an irregular shape
Pencil	Draws freehand lines one pixel wide	Ellipse	Draws a circle or oval
Brush	Draws freehand with selected size and shape	Rounded Rectangle	Draws a rectangle or square with rounded corners

Figure 4-8 Circle and square filled with color

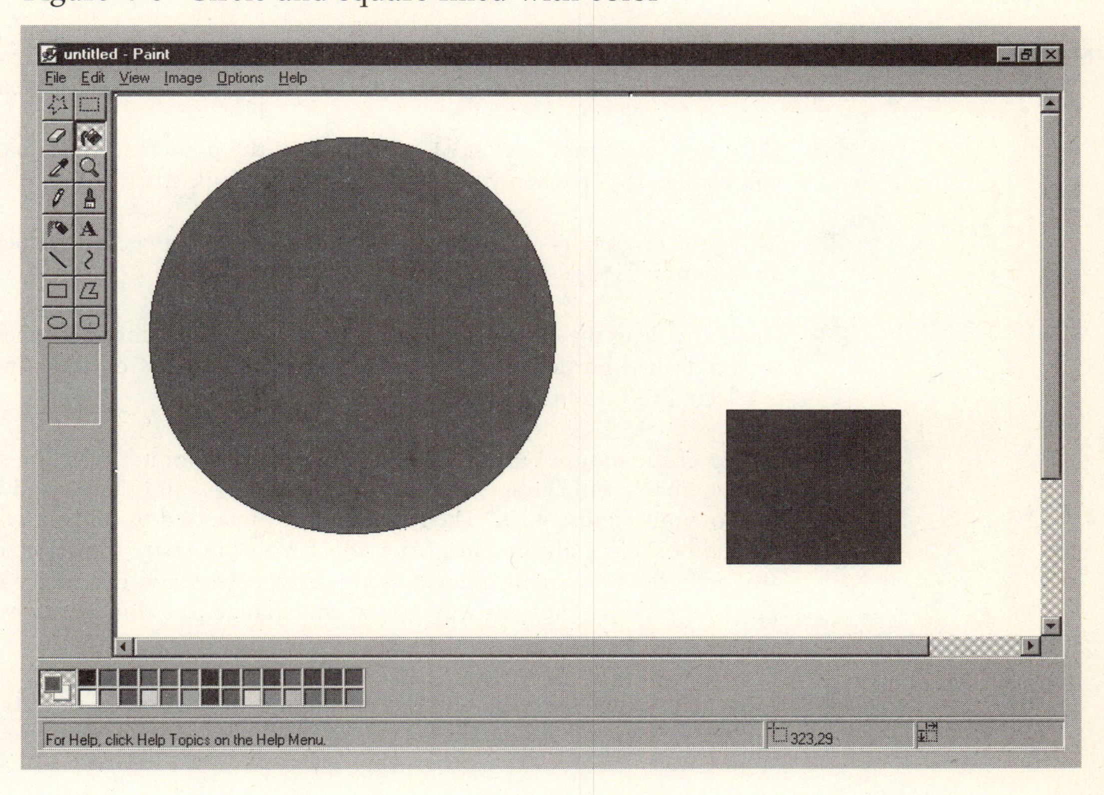

Practice

Open a new Paint document and draw seven shapes, alternating squares and circles of approximately the same size, and fill them with the colors of the rainbow.

Hot Tip

Double-clicking on a color will open a dialog box that allows you to edit that hue, creating your own custom color.

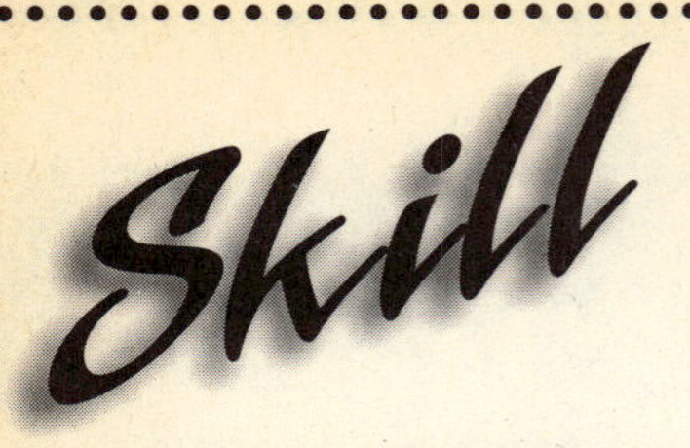

Advanced Paint Functions

Concept

Just as you can edit using a word processor, you can **alter a paint file**. Paint has tools that allow you to move shapes that you have drawn and also lets you add text to the file.

Do It!

Mike wants to move the square into the circle and add a line of text to his picture.

1. Click the **Select** tool button, then move the pointer to the square. The pointer will change to + when you move it onto the work space.

2. Move the crosshairs close to, but not touching, the upper left corner of the square, as shown in Figure 4-9.

3. Click and drag the crosshairs just past the lower right corner of the square. A box with a dashed border will appear around the square. Everything inside of this box is selected to be edited.

4. Let go of the mouse button. When you move the pointer over the selected figure, the crosshairs will change to a **four-way arrow** ✥, and the dashed box will appear as shown in Figure 4-10. The four-way arrow is used to move a selected area. The dashed box has eight **handles** from which you can resize the selected area. They are indicated by a small solid square in each corner and one in the middle of each side of the box. The four-way arrow will change to a **double arrow** when you are over one of the handles.

5. Move the pointer into the selected area and drag the square onto the middle of the circle. Click anywhere outside of the selected area to set the square into place. Figure 4-11 displays the square in the circle.

Figure 4-9 Items ready to be selected

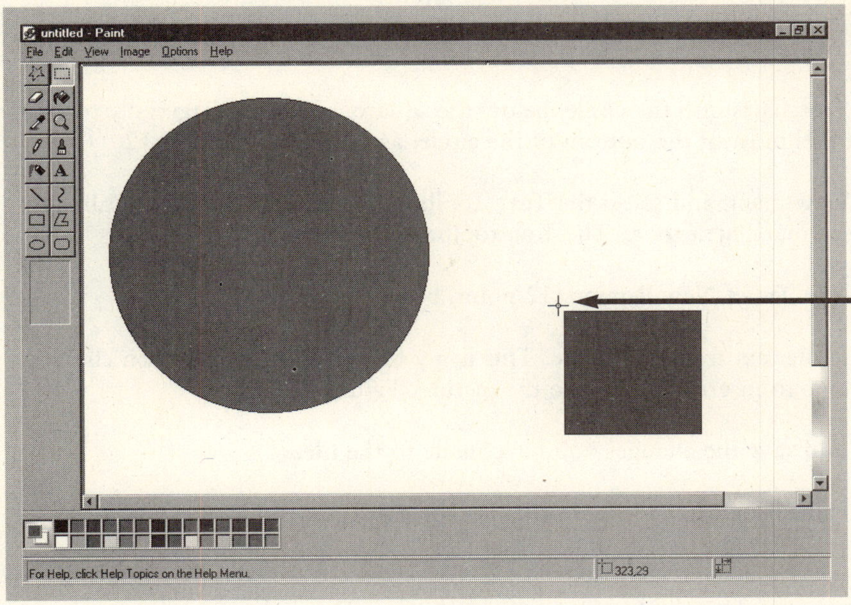

Figure 4-10 Selected object

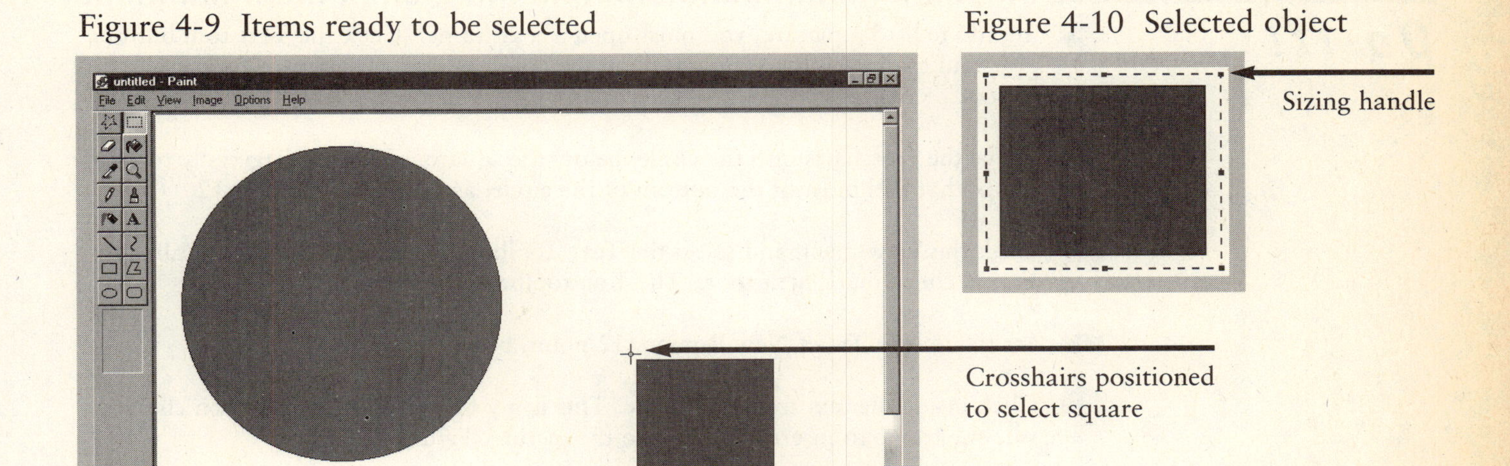

Figure 4-11 Square moved to the center of the circle

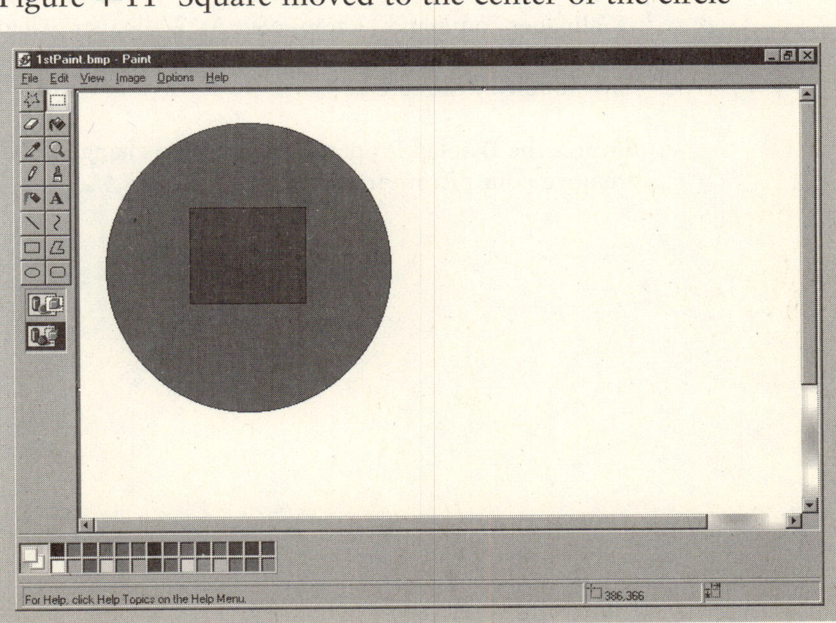

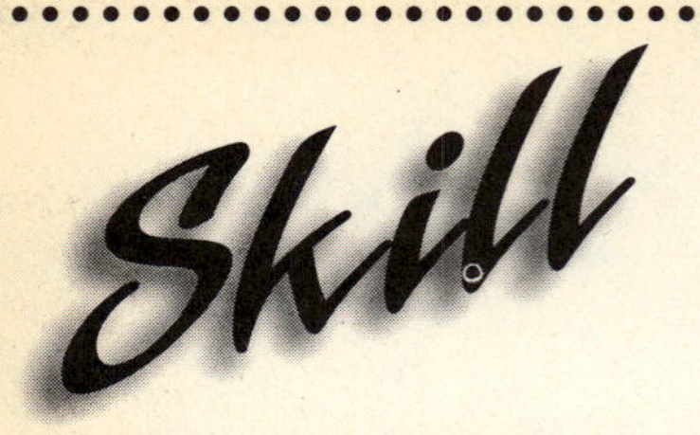

Advanced Paint Functions (continued)

Do It!

6. To add text to a picture, you must open a text frame. Click the **Text** tool button A, and then click the **yellow** box on the color palette. The text you type will be yellow.

7. Move the crosshairs into the circle, below the square, and drag diagonally to create a box that fills most of the bottom of the circle, as shown in Figure 4-12.

8. Click the **View** menu and select the **Text Toolbar** command if it does not already have a check mark next to it. The Text toolbar dialog box will open.

9. Set the text to **Times New Roman, 12 point, bold.**

10. Click inside the text frame and type, **This is my first paint picture**. Then click outside the frame to insert the text into the picture (Figure 4-13).

11. Click **File** and save the changes you have made to the file.

12. Close the Paint program by double-clicking the **control** menu icon.

More

Paint files are saved as graphic files called **bitmaps**. The desktop background you see is a bitmap. Therefore any file you create using Paint can be used as a background for your desktop.

The File menu in the Paint application contains two Set As Wallpaper commands. With your paint file open and saved, click the **File** menu and then select the **Set As Wallpaper** command. Choose Set As Wallpaper (Tiled) to cover the screen with repetitions of your bitmap or Set As Wallpaper (Centered) to place your picture in the middle of the screen.

Access the Display Properties window to change the desktop pattern if you wish to remove your picture from the desktop.

Figure 4-12 A text box

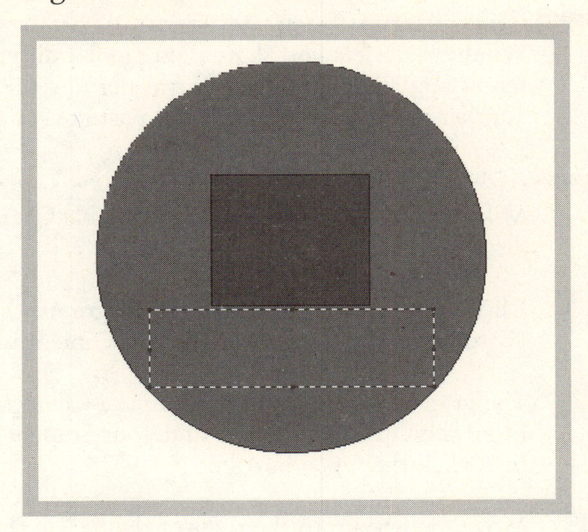

Figure 4-13 Text inserted

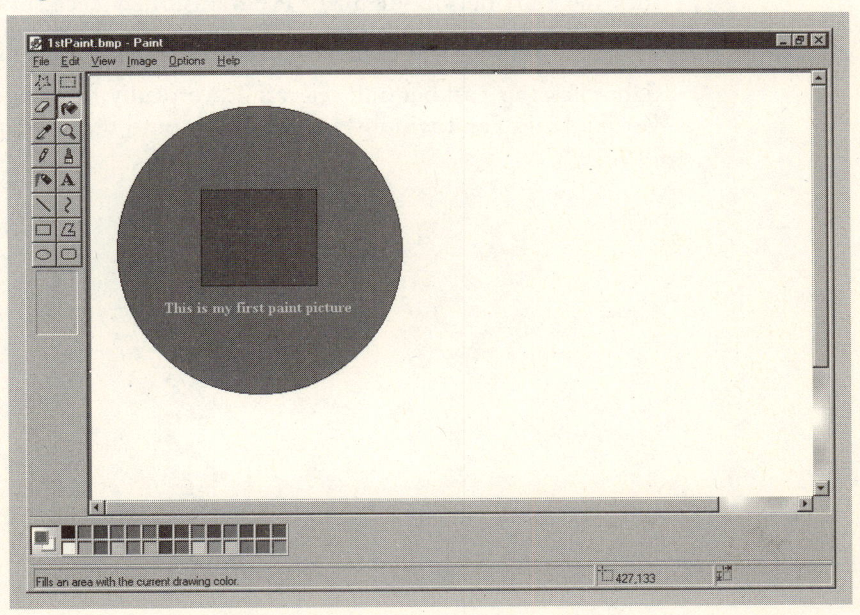

Practice

Open Prac4-6 from your Student Folder and follow the instructions on the screen.

Hot Tip

Use the Help Topics to learn more about Paint and its capabilities.

Sharing Data Between Applications

Concept

Windows 95 lets you **share data among different files**, even those created with different applications. You can transfer any file, whole or part, from one document to another using the cut, copy, and paste techniques you learned earlier in this lesson.

Do It!

Mike would like to add a graphic to his Client Letter. He will copy a Paint file directly into a WordPad document.

1. Click the **Start** button, highlight **Programs**, then **Accessories**, and select **WordPad.** WordPad will open with a blank document window.
2. The graphic is to be inserted into the Client Letter. Click the **Open** button. From the Open dialog box find your Student Folder, click the **Client Letter** file and then click the **Open** button.
3. Move the I-beam to the right of the "g" in the word "Shredding" in the letterhead. Click the mouse button to move the insertion point here, then press the **[Enter]** key to move the insertion point down one line. This is where you will paste the graphic.
4. Click the **Start** button, highlight **Programs**, then **Accessories**, and select **Paint**. Paint will open with a blank document window.
5. Right-click the **Taskbar** and select **Tile Vertically** from the pop-up menu. The WordPad and Paint windows will both fit onto the desktop as shown in Figure 4-14.

Figure 4-14 Paint and WordPad tiled vertically

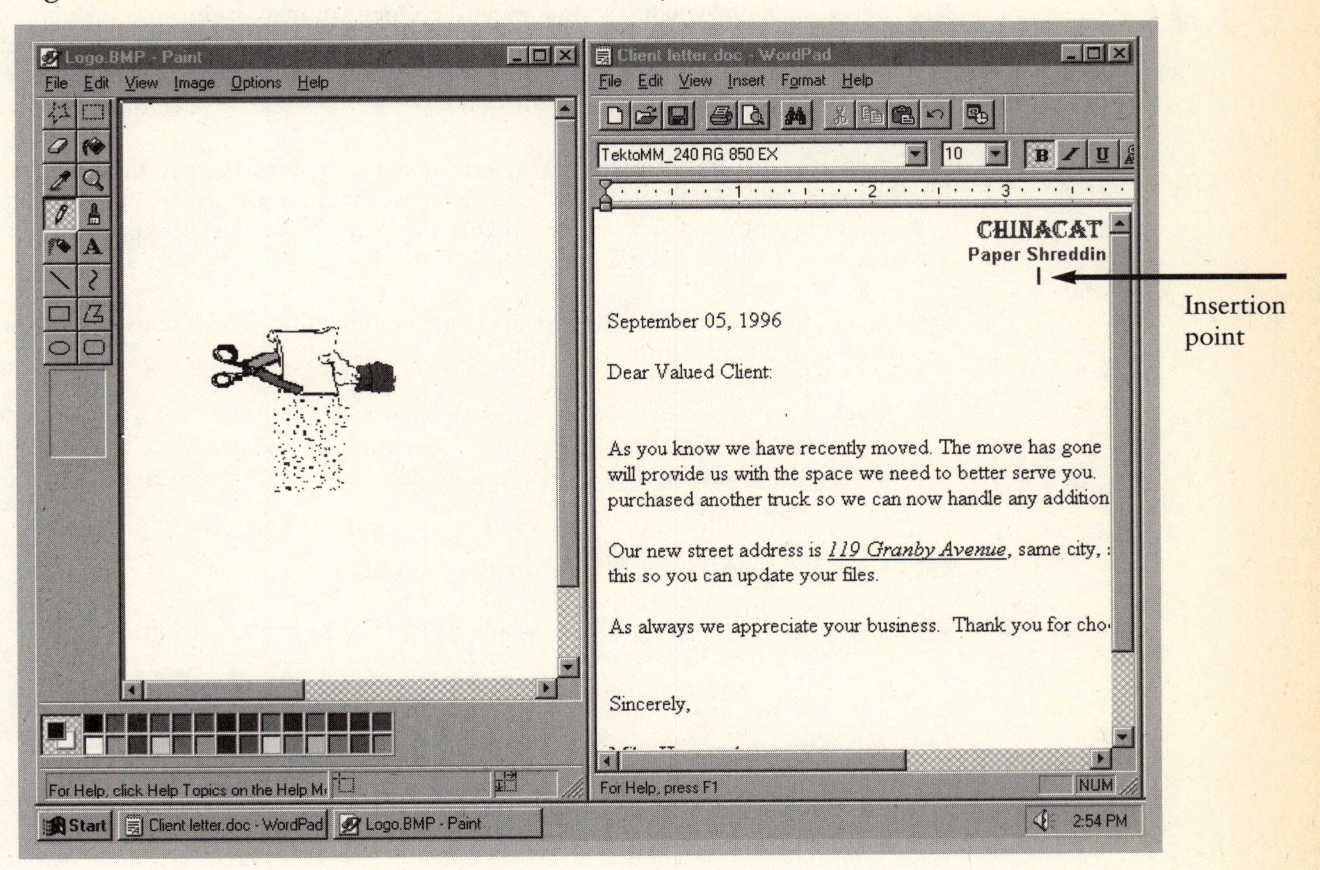

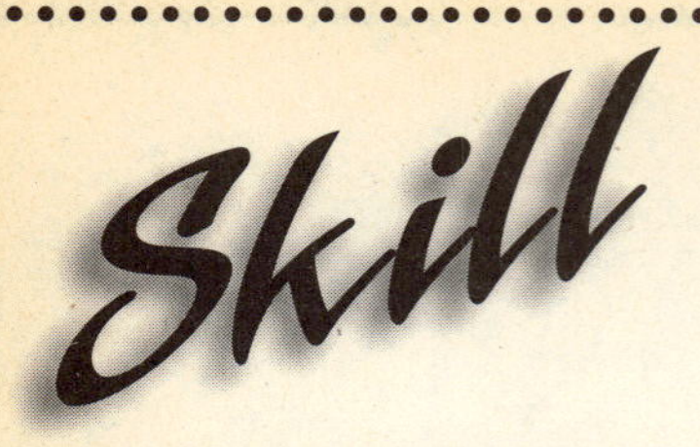

Sharing Data Between Applications (continued)

Do It!

6. Click the **Paint** File menu and select the **Open** command. From the Open dialog box find your student folder, click the Logo file, and then click the **Open** button. The Logo file will open in the Paint window. If you cannot see the entire picture use the scroll bars to bring it into view.

7. Click the **Select** tool button, and then use the crosshairs to drag a rectangle around the logo to select it. Try to form as small a rectangle as possible to encompass the entire logo. Click on a blank place on the work space if you need to clear the selection and open a new selection box.

8. Click the **Edit** menu and select the **Copy** command to send a copy of the selected area to the Clipboard.

9. Click **WordPad** to activate its window, then click the **Paste** button to insert the logo into the Client Letter (Figure 4-15). Click on a blank space to deselect the image, then maximize the WordPad window to see the document with the logo pasted into place.

10. Click the **Save** button to store the changes.

11. Close the WordPad and Paint windows by clicking the **Close** buttons.

Figure 4-15 Logo inserted into Client Letter

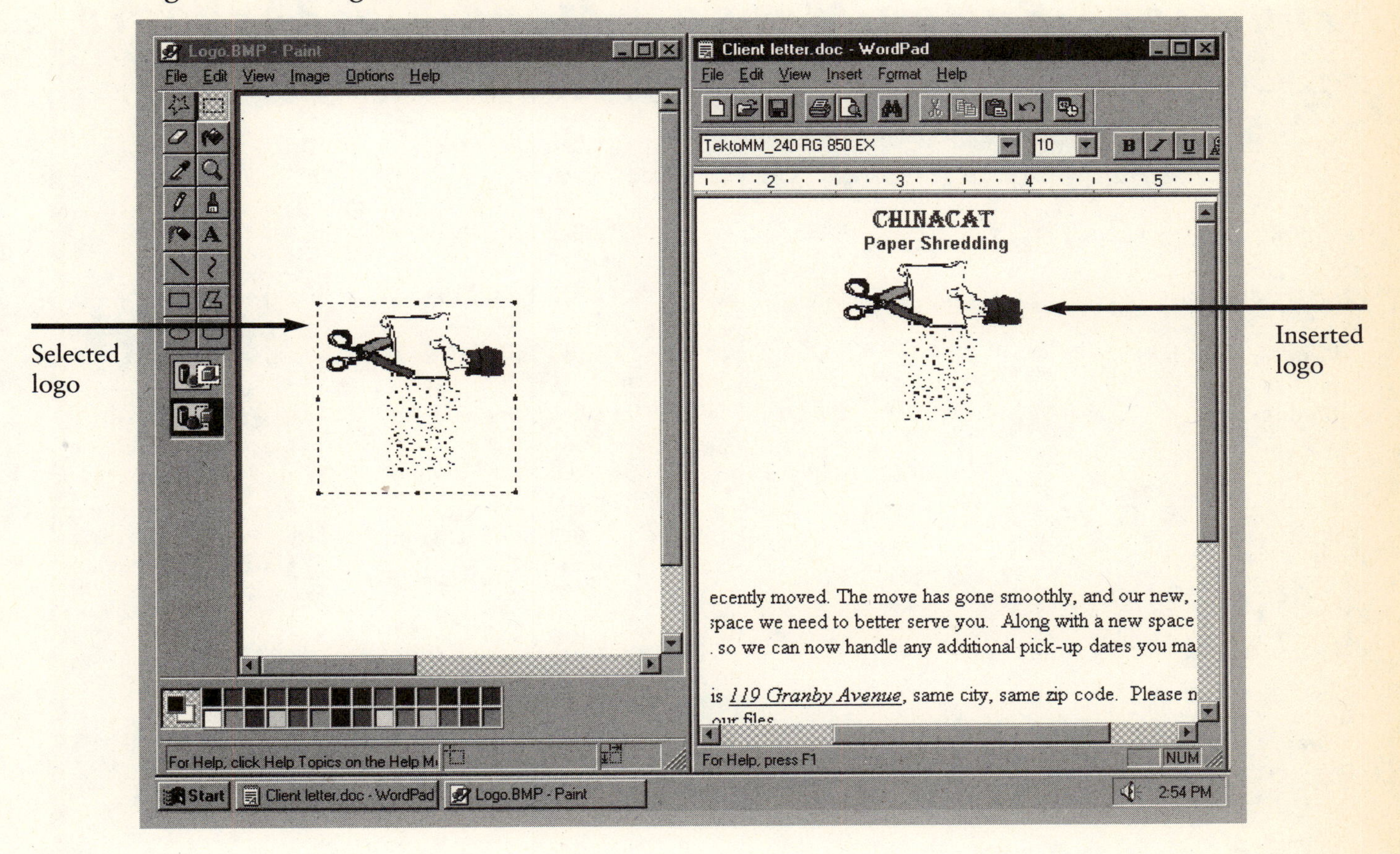

Practice

Open the file Prac4-7 and follow the on-screen instructions.

Hot Tip

Once you have selected a picture or text, the Cut, Copy, and Paste commands can be executed by right-clicking.

Shortcuts

Function	Button/Mouse	Menu	Keyboard
Open a file		Click File, Open	[Alt] + [F], [O]
Save a file		Click File, Save, or Save As	[Alt] + [F], [S] or [A]
Copy		Click Edit, Copy	[Ctrl] + [C]
Cut		Click Edit, Cut	[Ctrl] + [X]
Paste		Click Edit, Paste	[Ctrl] + [V]
Bold text	B	Click Format, Font, Bold, OK	[Alt] + [O], [F], [Alt] + [Y], arrow to Bold, [Enter]
Italicize text		Click Format, Font, Italic, OK	[Alt] + [O], [F], [Alt] + [Y], arrow to Italic, [Enter]
Underline text	U	Click Format, Font, Underline, OK	
Change font	Times New Roman	Select text, click arrow in font text box, click font	[Alt] + [O], [F], [Alt] + [F], arrow to font, [Enter]
Change font size	12	Select text, click arrow in font size text box, click font	[Alt] + [O], [F], [Alt] + [S], arrow to size, [Enter]
Undo changes		Click Edit, Undo	[Alt] + [E], [U]
Print		Click File, Print	[Ctrl] + [P]
Start a Program	Click Start button, point to Programs, click desired program		[Ctrl] + [S], arrow to program, [Enter]
Switch to another open program	Double-click the program button on the Taskbar		[Alt] + [Tab]
Exit a program	X	Click File, Exit	[Alt] + [F], [X]

Identify Key Features

Figure 4-16

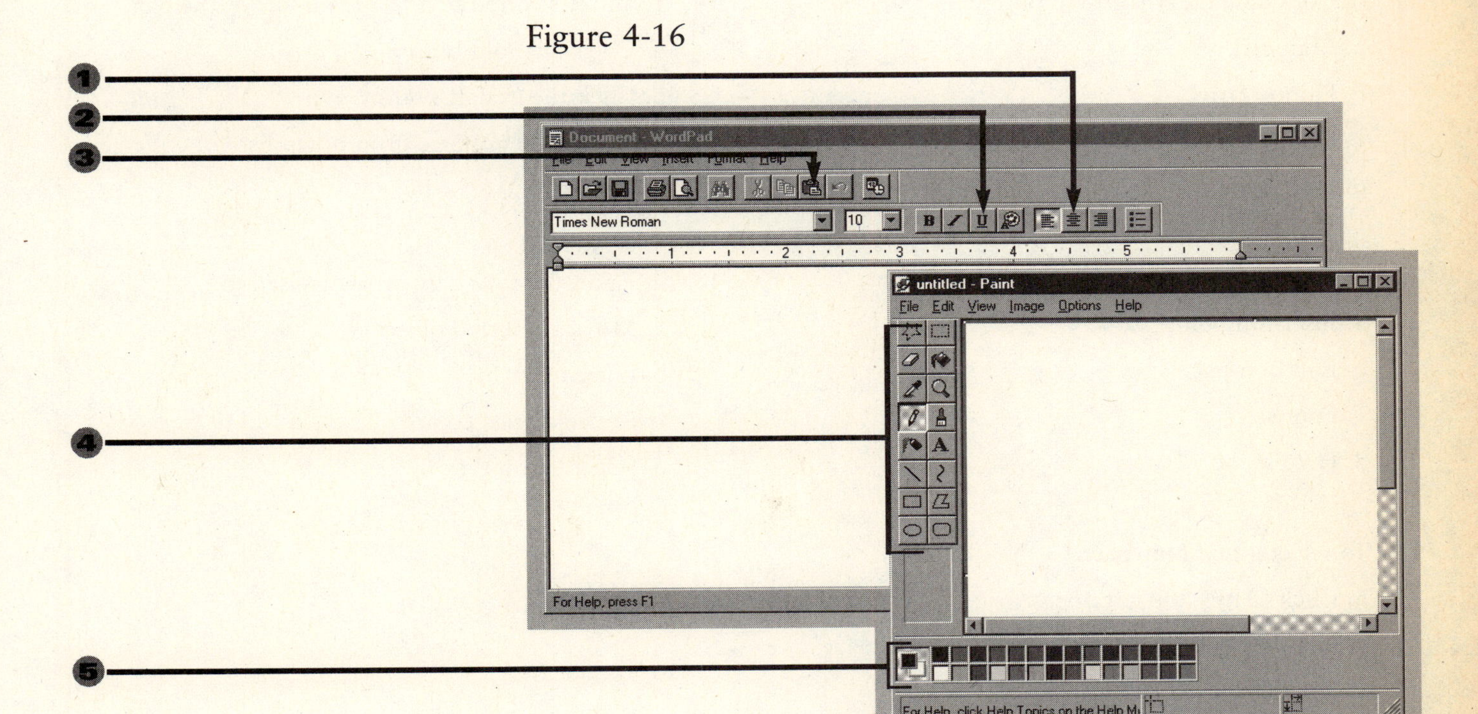

Select the Best Answer

6. Allows you to work with a file while keeping the original intact
7. Command that sends selected text to the Clipboard
8. Page orientation where the width is greater than the height
9. Transfers a file from your computer to paper
10. Application that is useful for creating and working with images

a. Cut
b. Landscape
c. Renaming
d. Paint
e. Printing

Quiz (continued)

Complete the Statement

11. Cut or copied text is stored on the:
    a. Maindisk
    b. Floppy Drive
    c. Clipboard
    d. Start menu

12. In WordPad a flashing cursor indicates the:
    a. Insertion point
    b. End of a page
    c. Font size
    d. Help menu

13. To select a text sentence:
    a. Click [Alt] + the left arrow
    b. Use the Select command from the Edit menu
    c. Double-click the Find button
    d. Drag the I-beam over the text

14. To move selected text to the middle of the page:
    a. Click the Bold button
    b. Click the Center button
    c. Click the Font Size drop-down list
    d. Press [Control] + [C]

15. In Paint, the four-way arrow is used to:
    a. Move a selected object
    b. Enter text
    c. Resize a selected area
    d. Select an object

Interactivity

Test Your Skills

1. Create and save a WordPad document:

   a. Open WordPad

   b. Enter the following text exactly as it appears here:

      True Brew

      According to the *Reinheitsgebot*, the German Beer Purity Law of 1516, beers are only permitted to contain four ingredients: water, barley, yeast, and hops. Water is the main component of beer, and the cleaner the water the better the beer. Barley adds flavor and color to a brew. Darker-roasted grains are used for ales and stouts, while lighter grains are added to lagers. Fermented yeast produces the acohol. Ales are made from top-fermenting yeast, and lagers are brewed with bottom-fermenting strains. Hops are what give beer its distinct bitter flavor. Hops were not an original ingredient of beer, but in the days before refrigeration, it was found that hopping the brew added to its shelf life. All other ingredients, such as corn or rice, are called adjuncts.

   c. Save the file as 1516 on your student disk.

2. Edit the WordPad document you just created:

   a. Correct the spelling of the word "acohol" by inserting an "l" between the "a" and the "c."

   b. Change the word "found," in the second to last sentence, to the word "discovered."

   c. Move the last sentence to make it the second sentence by using cut and paste commands.

3. Add formatting to a WordPad document:

   a. Center the words "True Brew" and change the font to 16 point Ariel.

   b. Italicize "German Beer Purity Law of 1516."

   c. Bold the words "water," "barley," "yeast," and "hops."

Interactivity (continued)

Test Your Skills

4. Work with Paint:
   a. Open Paint.
   b. Open the file named Test5.
   c. Fill the body of the stein with silver and the cap with maroon.
   d. Insert the Word "ALE" onto the mug.
   e. Draw a rounded square around the entire mug and fill it with green.
   f. Save the file under the name Stein.

5. Insert the mug into your WordPad document and print:
   a. Open Paint and WordPad.
   b. Right-click the Taskbar and Tile Vertically.
   c. Go to Paint and open a selection box around the picture.
   d. Send the picture to the Clipboard by copying.
   e. Click WordPad to activate the window.
   f. Move the insertion point to the right of the last word in the last sentence of your WordPad document, and then press the [Enter] key twice.
   g. Format the insertion point for centering.
   h. Paste the picture onto the bottom of your document.
   i. Print the document in Landscape orientation.

Interactivity (continued)

Problem Solving

As the newly elected president of the Seven Dollar Club, a group for avid movie fans, tradition dictates that by the next meeting you have to post a list of ten movies that you consider to be among the best ever made. You will use WordPad to create this list. You have also decided that the club needs a logo to use on all of its correspondence. Use Paint to make this logo and then insert it into your WordPad document.

1. Using WordPad, create a numbered list of the ten movies you consider to be the best ever made.
2. Using an 18-point font of your choosing, title the list "The Ten Greatest Movies Ever Made."
3. Center and bold the title.
4. Read your list and correct any errors that you may have made.
5. Using Paint, create a simple movie projector like the one shown in Figure 4-17. This projector can be drawn using the square, circle, and line tools.
6. Fill the body of the projector and the reels with the colors of your choice by clicking on the colors and using the Fill With Color tool.
7. Add the text "Seven Dollar Club" below the projector in 8 point Times New Roman.
8. Save the picture under the name Projector.
9. Insert the projector, centered, above the title line in your WordPad document using cut and paste techniques.
10. Save the WordPad file under the name Movies.

Figure 4-17

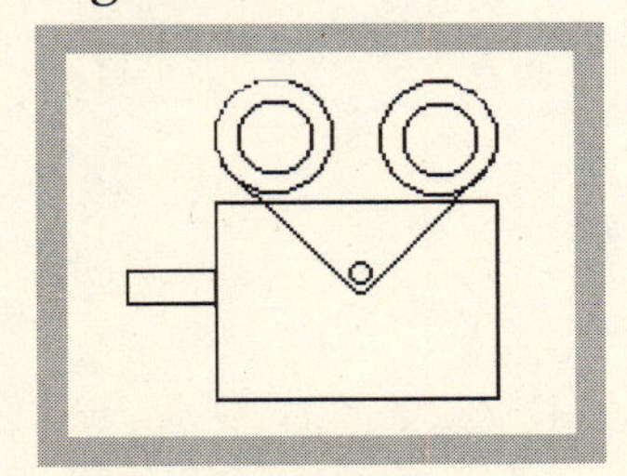

Glossary

A

Accessories
Programs built into Windows 95 that are useful for everyday tasks.

Active window
The window you are currently using. When a window is active, its title bar changes color to differentiate it from other open windows and its program button is depressed.

B

Background
The surface of the desktop on which icons and windows appear; you can customize its appearance by opening the Display Control Panel.

C

Cascade
Organizes open windows so that they overlap. The active window on top can be viewed in full, while only the title bars of the other windows can be seen.

Check box
A small square box that allows you to turn a dialog box option on or off by clicking it.

Click
To press and release a mouse button in one motion; usually refers to the left mouse button.

Clipboard
A temporary storage area for cut or copied text or graphics. You can paste the contents of the Clipboard into any Windows program, such as WordPad or Microsoft Word. The Clipboard holds the information until it is replaced with another piece of text, or until the computer is shut down.

Close
To quit an application and remove its window from the desktop. The Close button appears in the upper-right corner of a window, on the title bar.

Command
Directive that carries out an application feature or provides options for carrying out a feature.

Command button
In a dialog box, a button that carries out an action. A command button usually has a label that describes its action, such as OK, Cancel, or Help. If the label is followed by an ellipsis, clicking the button displays another dialog box.

Control menu
Contains commands relating to resizing, moving, and closing a window.

Control Panel
A utility used for changing a computer setting. You can access the various control panels through either the Start menu, My Computer, or the Explorer.

Copy
To place a duplicate of a file or portion thereof on the Clipboard to be pasted in another location.

Cursor
The blinking vertical line in a document window that indicates where text will appear when you type. Also referred to as the insertion point.

Cut
To remove a file, or a portion of a file, and place it on the Clipboard.

Cut and paste
To remove information from one place and insert it in another using the Clipboard as the temporary storage area.

D

Desktop
The on-screen area, created using the metaphor of a desk, that provides workspace for your computing tasks.

Dialog box
A box that explains the available command options for you to review or change before executing the command.

Document window
The window within the application window in which a file is viewed and edited. When the document window is maximized, it shares a border and title bar with the application window.

Double-click
To press and release the mouse button twice rapidly; usually refers to the left mouse button.

Drag
To hold down the mouse button while moving the mouse.

E

Edit
To add, delete, or modify elements of a file.

F

File
A document that has been created and saved under a unique file name.

File hierarchy
A logical order for folders and files that resembles how you would organize files and folders in a filing cabinet. Your file hierarchy displays where on your computer your folders and files are stored.

File management
The skill of organizing files and folders.

Folders
Subdivisions of a disk that work like a filing system to help you organize files.

Font
A name given to a collection of text characters of a certain size, weight, and style. Font has become synonymous with typeface. Arial and Times New Roman are examples of font names.

Format
The way information appears on a page. To format means to change the appearance of data without changing its content.

G

Graphical user interface (GUI)
An environment made up of meaningful symbols, icons, words, and windows that control the basic operation of a computer and the programs it runs.

H

Help button
A button in a Help window that opens a dialog box or a program to provide an answer to your question.

Highlight
When an item is shaded to indicate that it has been selected.

Horizontal scroll bar
Changes your view laterally when all of the information in a file does not fit in the window.

I

Icon
Pictorial representation of programs, files, and other screen elements.

Insertion point
A vertical blinking line on the screen that indicates where text and graphics will be inserted. The insertion point also indicates where an action will begin.

K

Keyboard shortcut
A keyboard equivalent of a menu command (e.g., [Ctrl] + [X] for Cut).

L

Landscape
A term used to refer to horizontal page orientation; opposite of "portrait," or vertical, orientation.

Launch
To start a program so you can work with it.

List box
A drop-down list of items. To choose an item, click the list box drop-down arrow, then click the desired item from the list.

M

Maximize
To enlarge a window to its maximum size. Maximizing an application window causes it to fill the screen; maximizing a document window causes it to fill the application window.

Menu
A list of related commands in an application.

Menu bar
Lists the names of menus containing application commands. Click a menu name on the menu bar to display its list of commands.

Minimize
To shrink a window to its minimum size. Minimizing an application window reduces it to a button on the Windows Taskbar; minimizing a document window reduces it to a short title bar in the application window.

Mouse
A palm-sized, hand-operated input device that you roll on your desk to position the mouse pointer and click to select items and execute commands.

Mouse buttons
The two buttons on the mouse, called the left and right mouse buttons, that you use to make selections and issue commands.

Mouse pointer
The usually arrow-shaped cursor on the screen that you control by guiding the mouse on your desk. You use the mouse pointer to select items, drag objects, choose commands, and start or exit programs. The appearence of the mouse pointer can change depending on the task being executed.

Multitasking
The ability to run several programs on your computer at once and easily switch among them.

My Computer
A tool used to view the files and folders that are available on your computer and how they are arranged. The default icon, a PC, appears on the desktop.

N

Network
Two or more computers linked together to allow for the sharing and exchanging of data.

O

Operating System
Controls the basic operation of your computer and the programs you run on it. Windows 95 is an operating system.

P

Pattern
A design that you can use to change the appearance of your desktop background.

Point
To place the mouse pointer over an item on the desktop.

Pop-up menu
The menu that appears when you right-click certain places in the Windows environment.

Portrait
A term used to refer to vertical page orientation; opposite of "landscape," or horizontal, orientation.

Program
A software application that performs specific tasks, such as Microsoft Word or WordPad.

Program button
The button that appears on the Taskbar to indicate that an application is open. The active program is represented by an indented button.

Properties
The characteristics of a specific element (such as the mouse, keyboard, or desktop display) that you can change. Properties can also refer to characteristics of a file such as its name, type, size, and location.

Radio button
A small circular button in a dialog box that allows you to switch between options.

RAM (random access memory)
The memory that programs use to function while the computer is on. When you shut down the computer, all information in RAM is lost.

Recycle Bin
An icon on the desktop that represents a temporary storage area for deleted files. Files will remain in the Recycle Bin until you empty it, at which time they are permanently removed from your computer.

Restore
To return the window to its previous size before it was resized (either Maximized or Minimized). A Restore button usually appears in the upper right corner of a window, on the title bar.

Right-click
To click the right mouse button; often necessary to access specialized menus and shortcuts. The designated right and left mouse buttons may be reversed with the Mouse control panel to accommodate user preferences.

Run
To open an application.

S

Screen saver
A pattern that fills your screen after your computer has been idle for a specified amount of time. The motion of a screen saver prevents images from being burned into the screen.

Scroll bar
A graphical device for moving vertically and horizontally through a document with the mouse. Scroll bars are located along the right and bottom edges of the document window.

Scroll bar box
A small gray box located inside a scroll bar that indicates your current position relative to the rest of the document window. You can advance a scroll bar box by dragging it, clicking the scroll bar on either side of it, or by clicking the scroll bar arrows.

Select
Highlighting an item to indicate that it is the active object on the screen. Usually done in order to perform some operation on the item.

Shortcut
A link that takes you directly to a particular file, folder, or program without having to pass through each item in its file hierarchy.

Shut down
The process you go through to turn off your computer when you finish working. After you complete this action it is safe to turn off your computer.

Start button
A button on the Taskbar that accesses a special menu that you use to start programs, find files, access Windows Help and more.

T

Taskbar
A bar, usually located at the bottom of the screen, that contains the Start button, shows which programs are running by displaying their program buttons, and shows the current time.

Text box
A rectangular area in which text is added so that it may be manipulated independently of the rest of a document.

Tile Horizontally
Organizes open windows so that they are stacked one on top of the other.

Tile Vertically
Organizes open windows so that they are arranged side-by-side.

Title bar
The horizontal bar at the top of a window that displays the name of the document or application that appears in the window.

Toolbar
A graphical bar containing buttons that act as shortcuts for common commands.

ToolTip
A small box displaying the name of a toolbar button that appears on your screen temporarily when you point to the button.

Triple-click
In some programs, performing this action is an easy way to select an entire line or block of text.

V

Vertical scroll bar
Moves your view up and down through a window, allowing you to view portions of a document that are not currently visible.

W

Wallpaper
An image in the format of a Windows 95 Paint files, bitmap (BMP), that can be displayed as your desktop background.

Window
A rectangular area on the screen in which you view and work on files.

Windows Explorer
A tool that allows you to view the hierarchy of folders on your computer and all the subfolders and files in a selected folder. Windows Explorer is very useful for moving and copying files among folders.

Index

Notes